AF412359

MUHAMMAD'S COMPANIONS:

ESSAYS ON SOME WHO BORE WITNESS TO HIS MESSAGE

Laleh Bakhtiar

© Library of Islam, 1993

All rights reserved. No part of this book may be reproduced or utilized in any form or by any means, electronic or mechanical, including photocopying and recording or by any information storage and retrieval system, without the written permission of the publisher. All inquiries may be sent to KAZI Publications, Inc.

Library of Congress Cataloging in Publication Data

Bakhtiar, Laleh
   Muhammad's Companions: Essays on Some Who Bore Witness to His Message

   Includes bibliographical references.
   1. Muslims—Companions—Biography
   BP75.L.56 1993 297'.63
   ISBN:1-56744-426-1

Published by:
Library of Islam
P. O. Box 1923
Des Plaines, IL 60017

Distributed by
KAZI Publications, Inc.
3023-27 W. Belmont Avenue
Chicago, IL 60618

CONTENTS

To those Muslims
who have lived their lives
bearing witness
to the
Message
of the
Prophet of Islam

PREFACE

The present work relates the lives of thirty-three companions, thirteen of whom are women, through the time line of early Islamic history. These essays on the lives of the companions bear witness to the major incidents in early Islam emphasizing the life of Prophet Muhammad and His Message. They begin with the time of revelation when Islam had to be practiced secretly in closed circles. It is then revealed to Prophet Muhammad to make the invitation to Islam public and to invite his near kin. The open invitation invites opposition by those who practice infidelity to the One God. Torture and persecution follow for some of the early companions. As the situation becomes unbearable, Prophet Muhammad tells those Muslims who wish to do so to migrate to Abyssinia. Then, a few years later, he himself migrates to Madinah. The migration marks the transition between the Makkah and Madinah periods of early Islamic history. Once in Madinah, Prophet Muhammad lays the foundation for an Islamic state to which his companions bore witness, some with words and others with their lives for the word *shahid* in Arabic means both.

This present collection, prepared for the secondary level student, comes from primary sources where very little is written about some and a great deal about others. The focus in this volume, however, is not so much a biography of their lives as much as showing how their lives bore witness to the Message of God's Messenger. The essays are based on when the most significant, most memorable events took place that highlight the witnessing of the message of that companion. For example, the highlight of bearing witness by Abu Bakr was the migration to Madinah and the events surrounding it. Hence, his name appears as eighteenth and not first or second. This reasoning is further elaborated in the Introduction. Each essay is followed by discussion questions and identifications.

It should be noted that the use of blessings on Prophet Muhammad and other prophets and his companions is common practice in Arabic, Persian, Turkish, and Urdu, but this is not common practice in the English language. As this book is for both English speaking Muslims and non-Muslims and in order not to become too cumbersome for the non-Muslim reader, whether any indication is given after reference to their names or not, a Muslim would send blessings with his/her heart. A method has been used here to indicate the blessing upon Prophet

Muhammad, peace and the mercy of God be upon him, with (ص) as a graphic symbol of the connection of his life to the Arabic language, the language in which God chose to reveal the Quran.

May this work help all people to understand the significance of the lives of the companions as models for us to follow as we, *insh Allah*, continue to bear witness to the Message and the Messenger. May Allah bless the Library of Islam for their support, Fereshteh Kunkel and Elizabeth Kunkel, my Quranic students at the Albuquerque Islamic School in New Mexico, for their astute comments, and Dr. Abdul Basit for his time and strenuous endeavors in reviewing the content.

INTRODUCTION

Islamic practice is based on two sources, the Quran and the Traditions (the sayings, actions, and practices of Prophet Muhammad). The basis for this is found in Prophet Muhammad's sermon to the people on his Farewell Pilgrimage, "....Oh people! As I have told you, I have left something to which, if you will hold fast, you will never fall into error—a clear Sign—the Book of God [the Quran] and the practice (*sunnah*) of His Prophet [Muhammad]. So heed well what I say."

The *sunnah* or Traditions of Prophet Muhammad were recorded by the companions who bore eye and ear witness to his life. Islamic history, therefore, has always placed great importance on their lives. They include the three groups of early Muslims: those who died before the migration, those who migrated from Makkah to Madinah (emigrants) and those who lived in Madinah and accepted Islam (helpers).

The earliest books describing the lives of the companions only included those people who actually interacted with Prophet Muhammad during his lifetime and referred to the companions in the context of the development of the life of Prophet Muhammad. This approach, which is adopted in this work, can be called the 'developmental' approach. Here an important incident in the life of Prophet Muhammad is seen through the eyes of a companion who shared it with him, thereby bearing witness to the truth that he spoke. This developmental approach, which is the earliest approach in Islamic history, is very much in contrast to what can be called the 'traditional' approach, an approach which was used in later works.

The traditional approach did two things. It changed the criteria for a person to be considered a companion and it emphasized a few of them who played important roles in Islamic history after the death of Prophet Muhammad. The criteria of inclusion of a companion in the developmental approach is based upon actual interaction with Prophet Muhammad during his lifetime in some important event in Islamic history.

The traditional approach broadened the base to include anyone who met Prophet Muhammad even if in a very brief meeting. At the same time it also selected out, for instance, the lives of the companions in order of their conversion to Islam and importance of their roles after the death of Prophet Muhammad. Among them were, for instance, companions who became the four rightly guided caliphs, Abu Bakr as-Siddiq,

Umar ibn Khattab, Uthman ibn Affan, and Ali ibn Abi Talib. This is to adopt an approach which concentrates on the first three years after the revelation when Islam was practiced in secret.

The developmental approach, on the other hand, pivots around the idea of the foundation of the Muslim community (*ummah*) through the lives of the companions as they bore witness to the Message throughout the lifetime of Prophet Muhammad. Here all—men, women, and children—are considered important founding members of the community (*ummah*). The very diversity of the lives of the early companions, in their attempt to model the life of Prophet Muhammad, allows each and every Muslim to sense a connection between their own life and the life of one of the companions. This, then, strengthens their sense of unity as part of the community (*ummah*) that continues to bear witness to the message of Islam.

Bearing witness is an important concept in Islam and it appears many times in the Quran. The last time that Prophet Muhammad refers to it himself is in his sermon at the Farewell Pilgrimage. This is referred to in the last essay of this collection on the life of his beloved wife, A'ishah, who was a transmitter of Traditions of this event. During Prophet Muhammad's sermon, he asks the people, among whom are many of the early companions, "Oh people, have I conveyed [the Message]?" The people said, "Oh God, yes," and Prophet Muhammad said, "Oh God, bear witness!"

Beginning with *"God bears witness that there is no god but He,"* (3:18) to when God took the seed from the loin of the Children of Adam and asked, *"'Am I not your Lord?' They said, 'Yea. We do bear witness,'"* (7:172) the concept of bearing witness is an extremely important one in Islam. In verse 4:166, God says, *"God bears witness to what He has sent down to you [Muhammad]; He has sent it down with His knowledge; and the angels also bear witness; and God suffices for a witness."* That is, He also bears witness.

The believers are told, *"and that the Messenger might be a witness to you,"* (2:143) and *"Oh believers, be you securers of justice, witnesses for God."* (4:79) The People of the Book are reprimanded, *"Why do you disbelieve in God's Signs which you yourselves witness?"* (3:70) All human beings are told, *"their eyes and their skin bear witness against them,"* (41:20) referring to the Day of Judgment. The message of witnessing extends to the Muslim Community (*ummah*), as well, *"Thus We have made of you a Community (ummah) justly balanced that you might be witnesses over the nations, and the Messenger a witness over yourselves..."* (2:143).

The essays in this collection have been written with this perspective in mind. The companions were those human beings— men, women, and children—who bore witness to Prophet Muhammad's life. The lives of the companions are seen in the context of his life which falls into two major periods: CE 570-622 known as the Makkan period and CE 622-632 (AH 1-11) known as the Madinah period, bridged by the migration. The first essays are placed in Makkah and show the early years of Islam to which the companions bore witness. Many of them would become known as the emigrants when they migrated to Madinah. Many like Khadijah and Sumayyah did not live long enough to receive that blessing. A summary of each story in this volume follows.

The collection begins with **Khadijah,** the first person to accept the Message of Prophet Muhammad as she bore witness. The first three years the message was delivered secretly. When Arqam ibn Abi Arqam accepted Islam, he opened his home on the Safa hill to Prophet Muhammad to preach to the early Muslims in the privacy of his home. **Abu Dharr Ghifari** accepted Islam at this time as he bore witness. Barakah was entrusted with a message from Khadijah to Prophet Muhammad. We move through the thoughts and feelings she may have had as she passed through the streets of Makkah with her message. She had been the slave of Prophet Muhammad's father, Abdullah, and lived with his mother, Aminah, until Aminah died. **Barakah** then went to live with the family of Prophet Muhammad's grandfather. It is through her walk from one house to the other, as she bore witness, that we get a sense of what the people, who scorned his message, were saying about Prophet Muhammad. It was the direct result of this journey that she re-married.

Abdullah ibn Mas'ud was another early convert. He was the first after Prophet Muhammad to recite the Quran in the Kabah, as he bore witness, so that the idol worshippers could not deny having heard the revelation. Then the next series of lives of the companions are those who suffered the torture and persecution of the idol worshippers, as they bore witness, because under the tribal system prevalent among the pagan Quraysh, a person who had no tribe to protect him or her, was subject to abuse. These companions include **Sumayyah, Bilal,** and **Khabbab.**

The pressure upon Prophet Muhammad was great indeed as he daily observed the torture of his followers. The conversion of **Umar ibn Khattab** to Islam, as he bore witness, added great weight to the Muslim cause. The Quraysh idolaters considered it to be a real loss to themselves.

An important message that Prophet Muhammad brought is the

Islamic view of the human being to whom the message is directed. The Makkah period was the time of individual self-development in the *din* for the companions. They bore the brunt of the idol worshippers outrage against the message, "Say: 'God is One,' and be saved." This time of self-development and immersion in faith appealed to very different types of people. It shows the universality of Islam that there is to be no class, tribal, racial, or gender separation. The message of Islam is for one and all. The lives of some of the early converts—**Umm Dharr, Mus'ab ibn Umayr, Abdullah ibn Umm Maktum, Salim the Freed Slave** and **Tufayl ibn Amr al-Daws**—all bore witness to this.

Then in CE 615, unable to bear the torture of his followers, Prophet Muhammad gave the option to those who wanted to migrate to Abyssinia in order to avoid the pressure being applied against them in Makkah. **Miqdad ibn Amr al-Aswad** and **Ja'far ibn Abi Talib** were among the companions who bore witness to his message and migrated there.

In Makkah, the idol worshippers decided to impose economic sanctions on the Hashim and Abd al-Muttalib clans in an attempt to force Prophet Muhammad to give up his preaching. The years CE 617-620 were three years of hunger and thirst for Prophet Muhammad and his clans who had all moved, under the direction of Abu Talib, Prophet Muhammad's uncle, to a valley outside of Makkah. The confinement has been seen through the witnessing of **Fatimah bint Asad**, the wife of Abu Talib.

Finally, by CE 622, Prophet Muhammad had prepared the Muslims to be accepted in Madinah. He had been warned that the idolaters would try to kill him. He placed **Ali ibn Abi Talib** in his bed who thereby bore witness as Prophet Muhammad escaped in the middle of the night with his traveling companion on the migration, **Abu Bakr ibn Abi Quhafah**. The essay on Ali concerns his role in that event while the essay on Abu Bakr, as he bore witness, centers on the migration to Madinah. The two traveling companions, Prophet Muhammad and Abu Bakr, were aided in this migration by Abu Bakr's daughter, **Asma bint Abu Bakr** and her story as she bore witness follows.

Once they reached Quba, Prophet Muhammad ordered a mosque to be built and the essay on **Ammar ibn Yasir,** who became the master builder for this mosque as well as for the one in Madinah, reflects this period of the life of Prophet Muhammad. Once in Madinah, not all of the members of the clans of the two major tribes, the Aws and Khazraj, immediately accepted Islam. The essay on **Abu Darda al-Ansari al-Khazraj,** tells of his conversion, as he bore witness, through the effect of the Madinah Constitution, the world's first written Constitution. This marks the beginning of the phase of social and political development of the Islamic state.

Prophet Muhammad always remained close to his daughters. The essays on two of his daughters, **Fatimah bint Muhammad** and **Zaynab bint Muhammad**, show very different ways of life. Fatimah and her husband, Ali ibn Abi Talib, both early converts to Islam, received a gift from Prophet Muhammad, as they bore witness, when the daily struggle of life raising small children with not enough food to eat became too much for her. The essay on Zaynab, on the other hand, describes how after the first major battle of the Muslims against the idolaters, the Battle of Badr in CE 624, she was caught between being a Muslim herself while her husband was still an idolater. Prophet Muhammad's patience with her husband proved fruitful when he finally converted to Islam after he had to give up his wife.

In CE 625 the Muslims again had to fight against the Quraysh idolaters and in this battle, the Battle of Uhud, one of the greatest warriors of Islam, **Hamzah ibn Abd al-Muttalib**, the beloved uncle of Prophet Muhammad, bores witness when his witnessing became his martyrdom. The essay describes this and the concept of martyrdom in Islam. Women helped in the battles as nurses like **Humarah bint Jahsh ibn R'ab** through whom we see some of the social laws revealed in the Madinah period that she and her husband, as believers, would have witnessed and **Safiyyah bint Abd al-Muttalib**, through whom we learn more of the rights of believing women as revealed in the Quran.

The essay on **Salman Farsi** describes the role he played in building a trench in preparation for the Battle of the Confederates in April, CE 627 (AH 5) as his role in witnessing. Then the hostage incident of the Treaty of Hudaybiah is seen through the life of **Uthman ibn Affan** who willingly went on behalf of Prophet Muhammad in March CE 628 (AH 6) to negotiate with the idolaters. **Umm Salamah** also had an important role to play after the signing of the Treaty in March CE 628 (AH 6).

In CE 628-629 (AH 7), Prophet Muhammad sent out letters to heads of states inviting them to Islam. The responsibility of one courier to carry a letter is described in the life of **Abdullah ibn Hudhayfah**'s bearing witness. After the Battle of Khaybar in May-June, CE 628 (AH 7), Umm Habibah, the daughter of Abu Sufyan, joined Prophet Muhammad, who had married her some years before when her husband died an apostate. The marriage to Prophet Muhammad was arranged through a representative of the Prophet's as **Umm Habibah** stayed some time in Abyssinia following her marriage to Mustafa.

The story of the Battle of Mut'ah in September CE 629 (AH 8) is told through the life of one of the martyrs, **Zayd ibn Haritha**, as he bore witness with his life. Then in March CE 631 (AH 10), Prophet Muhammad performed the Farewell Pilgrimage. Many of the events of that pilgrimage are recorded in Traditions from his beloved wife, **A'ishah bint Abu Bakr**. The essay on her role as a transmitter of Traditions, as a way that she bore witness, is seen in the last essay of this volume.

KHADIJAH BINT KHUWAYLID:
The First Muslim Believer

It was CE 610. The Arabian peninsula was immersed in idol worship, having deviated far from the message of the Prophets of previous time and, in particular, from the message of the founder of monotheism (*tawhid*), Abraham, peace be upon him.

Khadijah, a wealthy widow, married to Muhammad for fifteen years, was awaiting his return home. As she waited, she recalled her marriage to him. It all began when she heard of Muhammad's character—his honesty, truthfulness, and trustworthiness. She had sent for him and asked if he would take her merchandise to Syria. He had agreed and she had sent her servant, Maysarah, with him.

She recalled that when they returned, Maysarah had told her of the virtuous qualities he had seen in Muhammad on this journey. Listening to Maysarah, Khadijah had felt very attracted to the good character and inner strength about which all who knew

1

Muhammad spoke. She remembered asking a woman friend of hers named Nufaysah to find out if Muhammad would be interested in marrying her as she was fifteen years older than he.

Nufaysah had gone to Muhammad and asked him why he did not marry. "I have not the means to marry," was his reply.

"What if you were given the means and you would marry beauty, nobility, and abundance? Would you then consent?" Nufaysah asked.

"Who is she?" Muhammad asked.

"Khadijah," Nufaysah responded.

"How could such a marriage be mine?" he asked.

"Leave it to me," Nufaysah responded.

"For my part," he said, "I am willing."

Nufaysah had told Khadijah of her conversation with Muhammad. Khadijah had then sent for Muhammad once again. She said to him, "Oh son of my uncle, I like you because of the high regard others have of you. People always speak of your trustworthiness, good character, and truthfulness." Then she proposed marriage. He accepted and they agreed to each speak to their respective uncles. Both sides were pleased with the idea and so they were married. From this marriage, Khadijah was to bear Muhammad six children. The first, Qasim, died before he was two. The next four were daughters, Zaynab, Umm Kulthum, Ruqayyah, and Fatimah. The sixth child, Tahir, had been a son who only lived for a short time.

Throughout the first fifteen years of their marriage, Khadijah recalled she had watched her beloved husband's torment and anguish as he suffered for the life of his people who lived in darkness and ignorance, worshipping idols that they themselves had carved — Lat, Uzza, Manat. He often shared with her his concern for people's worship of these stone and wooden forms. He also told her of being troubled by the poverty and oppression of his people.

Khadijah vividly remembered that during that time when he had sensed he was surrounded by the darkness of oppression, he had retreated to a cave on Mount Hira outside Makkah. Perhaps in prayer, perhaps in meditation, he had told her, a dawn would appear which would bear witness to a new order. He had sensed the silence before the storm. Perhaps history was planning to rebel against this status quo, against the oppressed—both the One God and His Abrahamic people.

As Khadijah awaited his return this day, he sat in the cave, lost in meditation deep and mystical, when suddenly he was to tell her that he had a true vision which only a Prophet can have. The angel of revelation, Gabriel, appeared to him and said, "Recite (*'iqra*)!" In surprise, he asked, "What shall I recite?" Once again and yet again, "Recite." And then Gabriel said, *"Recite in the Name of Your Lord Who created. He created the human being from a clot. Recite and Your Lord is most honorable, who taught (to write) with the pen, taught the human being what he knew not."* (95:1)

Deeply stirred, he rushed home to his beloved wife, Khadijah. She accepted him and what he said with certainty of belief. She knew he spoke the truth. She was the first convert to the faith: one who submits (*muslim*) to the Will of the One God (*islam*). The invitation of Abraham had re-asserted itself among a people who had forgotten the message of monotheism (*tawhid*), "there is no deity but God."

She said to him, "Rejoice, oh son of my uncle and be of good heart. Verily by Him in whose hand is Khadijah's soul, I had hoped that you would be the Prophet of these people."

Khadijah felt awed by the experience of which she sensed she was a part. She so loved Muhammad (ﷺ) that she deeply felt whatever happened to him. She felt honored to have been his wife when he first received the revelation; she respected his message and his mission. She offered him everything she had "upon the Way of God," asking for nothing in return.

Those who understand not her inner joy only see her bearing sorrow, poverty, and insults. They cannot comprehend the inward strength that grew strong and firm because she had placed her whole being upon His Way; dedicated her every asset for His cause. How blessed was this beloved Companion of God's Prophet to have been present at a moment of uncertainty in the life of Mustafa (the Chosen One) and to have had the discernment (*furqan*) to know it is the truth. Praise belongs to God (*al-hamd Allah*).

Upon hearing the news of the revelation to her beloved Muhammad (ﷺ), Khadijah went to the home of her cousin, Waraqah ibn Naufal. He was a Christian, a man learned in both the Torah and the Gospel, who had become blind with age. When she told him of what had happened, Waraqah cried out, "Holy! Holy! Verily in whose hand is Waraqah's soul, if you have spoken the truth to me, Khadijah, there has come unto him the greatest of angels, Gabriel, who came to Moses beforehand. Lo! He is the Prophet of this people. Bid him be of good heart." Khadijah returned to Muhammad and told him what her cousin had said.

Soon after that Muhammad (ﷺ) went again to the cave for a retreat and afterwards he circumambulated the Kabah. While he was doing this, he met Waraqah who asked him, "Oh son of my brother, tell me what you have seen and heard?" The Prophet told him and Waraqah said, "Surely by Him in whose hand is Waraqah's soul, you are the Prophet of these people. The greatest of the angels, Gabriel, has come to you as he came to Moses. You will be called a liar and you will be despised. They will cast you out and fight against you. Verily if I live to see that day, God knows I will help His Cause." Then he leaned forward and kissed the Messenger's forehead.

The words of comfort and reassurance from his beloved Khadijah and her cousin, Waraqah, were followed by a second revelation to the Prophet. It was not recorded exactly how this revelation came but the Messenger mentioned generally two ways by which he received revelation: "Sometimes it comes to me like the reverberations of a bell and that is the hardest upon me; the reverberations stop when I am aware of their message. And sometimes the Angel takes the form of a human being and speaks to me and I am aware of what he says."

The second revelation began with a single letter, *nun*. It was followed by one of the many oaths or things that God swears by in this and later verses. Here it was the pen which had already been mentioned in the first revelation as the primary means by which God teaches men His wisdom. When asked about the pen, the Prophet said, "The first thing God created was the pen. He created the tablet and said to the pen: 'Write,' and the pen answered, 'What shall I write?' God said, 'Write My knowledge of My creation until the Day of Resurrection.' Then the pen traced what had been commanded."

Then following the oath, *'by the pen'* comes *'by that which they write'*. These both are then followed by divine reassurance. "*Nun. By the pen and that which they write. You are not, by the grace of your Lord, mad or possessed. Nay, verily for you is a reward unfailing and you (stand) on an exalted standard of character.*" (68:1-4).

After the first two revelations, there came a period of silence to the extent that the Prophet began to fear that he had somehow incurred God's displeasure, although Khadijah continued to tell him that this was not possible. The silence was then broken and there came a further reassurance and with it, the first command directly related to his mission: "*By the glorious morning light and by the night when it is still. Your guardian Lord has not forsaken you nor is He displeased. And verily the Hereafter will be better for you than the present. And soon will your Guardian-Lord give you (that wherewith) you shall be well-pleased. Did he not find you an orphan and give you shelter? And He found you in need and made you independent. Therefore, treat not the orphan with harshness nor repulse the petitioner (unheard). But the bounty of your Lord—rehearse and proclaim*" (93:1-11).

Khadijah lived through the first ten years of the revelation in

Makkah. This was a time when the shorter surahs of the Quran had been revealed. Khadijah had been able to share in the joy and blessings of the revelations as the Prophet received them. Then, after twenty-five years as the only wife of God's Messenger, she died at the age of sixty-five having suffered through the three years of political confinement and economic sanctions by the idol-worshipping Quraysh of Makkah in the valley of Abu Talib. May Allah rest her soul in peace.

IDENTIFICATIONS:
* Maysarah
* Nufaysah
* Waraqah ibn Naufal
CONSIDER AND DISCUSS:
1. What is the significance of the first revelation?
2. What about Arab culture before Islam distressed the Messenger of God (ص)?

ABU DHARR GHIFARI:
He Walks Alone, Dies Alone, and Will Be Resurrected Alone

Muhammad (ﷺ) was in the home of Arqam ibn Abi Arqam on the hill of Safa, not far from the hill of Marwah in Makkah. A guide in front led in the darkness of the night and Jundub, the son of Junadah Ghifari followed behind him. They climbed Safa towards Muhammad (ﷺ). It seemed as if this was all part of a beautiful scene, a wonderful dream that held the key to their destiny. Step by step Abu-Dharr-to-be grew closer and, breath by breath, more restless; faith and certainty had conquered him. He would not return to his tribe until he saw the man who claimed to be a Messenger, knew him, and tested him. He had an appointment to see his heart's beloved and his faith's desire.

Now he was a few steps from the home of Arqam. What difficult moments! Bearing the first moments of the visit is serious. Love had captured Jundub. The son of Junadah was filled with "him." There was more "Muhammad" in him than himself. The son of Junadah was no more than a far distant and forgotten memory in the mind of Jundub. His heart had been placed in the magnetic field of a powerful force. Every moment a familiar aroma quickened his sense of smell and at this very moment he sensed the gravity of Muhammad's existence with all of his being. The Messenger's presence filled the area around Safa. Jundub knew who Muhammad was. He knew what he was saying , but ... what was he like? His face? His form? His way of speaking? His existence? How could he look at him? How could he speak to him? What would he say to him? What will be? What will happen?

"*As-salam alayk* (peace be upon you)."

"*Alayka salam wa rahmat Allah* (and upon you and the mercy of God)."

And these were the first greetings offered in Islam.

We do not know how long this visit took. Even if history had told us we would not know because time is of no avail at moments like these. That which we do know was that the son of Junadah descended into the house of Arqam and was lost there. No one knows to where he disappeared, but he was suddenly transformed from a bare-footed bedouin, poverty-stricken, desert dweller, who was a member of the "nameless mass" which history is too ashamed to record, into an Abu Dharr Ghifari. He was a man who was later to confront Mu'awiyyah—the man who unjustly seized the caliphate from the rightly-guided (*rashidin*) with force so that Muslims would be obliged to serve him—"Oh Mu'awiyyah! If you are building your palace with your own money, it is extravagance and if with the money of the people, it is treason."

The now-Abu-Dharr left the house of Arqam which was near the Kabah. He appeared upon the morning horizon of Islam, standing upon the summit of Safa, having just left the hiding place of revelation. Kindled by the dawn, he stopped for a moment. With eyes filled with the flame of the fire of the desert, Abu Dharr turned towards the mountainous walls of the valley of Makkah and held his look upon the idols of the Kabah. "These stupid statues have all guaranteed their carver-worshippers the satanic desire for monopoly, exclusivity, and arrogance which comes with considering yourself better than others." Abu Dharr had never seen things in this way before. He asked himself in indignant anger, "What are these three hundred and some deities, gods, idols doing in the house of the One God of Abraham?"

He hurriedly descended from Safa, a migrant, alone, set afire and determined. Abu Dharr had been asked to leave Makkah without hesitating to return to the Ghifar and to await the command, but the bony, frail breast of this "child of the wilderness" was weaker than to be able to hide such a fire within himself. Instead he became rebellion itself. He could not remain quiet. *"God charges no soul save to its capacity."* (2:286)

He stood in front of the Kabah, face to face with frightening idols, beside the Dar al-Naduh, the Quraysh senate, and shouted out the cry of his belief in the One God; he announced his belief in the mission of Muhammad (ص); he called the idols "mute stones which the people themselves had carved."

And this was the cry which Islam brought from a Muslim who outwardly rebelled against paganism and multitheism (*shirk*). The answer of multitheism was clear—death!— a death that will be a lesson for others. Without hesitation they fell upon him and pounded his head, face, breast, and sides in fury. Abbas came. The uncle of the Messenger was a usury collector and still of the same class as the pagan Quraysh aristocrats. Still driven by tribal loyalty, yet now for the right reason, he frightened his fellow Quraysh idol-worshippers, "This man is from the Ghifar tribe. If you kill him, the Ghifar swords will take out their revenge against your caravans." They must decide between their religion and their material world, deity or goods? A qiblah of love or caravan of money. Which? They pulled back without hesitation.

Abu Dharr tried to get up. The diameter of the circle of idol-worshippers around him grew larger. He got up. He supported himself on his own two feet. The crowd became more dense; it was as if they sought refuge in each other. Clearly coercion and compulsion feared faith here. He was one face and they were faceless, personality-less, each alone and all without identity. They were confronted by a human being, a person, a person to whom faith had given meaning, substance, ideals, orientation, and a wonderful, miracle-like, invincible power that the fearless dying for His Cause—martyrdom—grants to a believer.

Abu Dharr brought all of his family and, little by little, all of his tribe to Islam. He was with the Ghifar when the Muslims passed through the difficulties of the struggle in Makkah, when they undertook the migration, and, when in Madinah, they moved from the stage of self-development to the stage of founding a social system, as a consequence of which confrontations began.

It was here that Abu Dharr sensed that he should be on the scene. He went to Madinah and there, as he had no place or work, he made the Messenger's mosque his home—which at that time was the home of the people—and he joined the *Saffah* (Porch) Companions. He sacrificed living for ideology, serving the movement—in times of peace—with thought, knowledge, and prayer and—in times of war—with war.

Islam, under the leadership of the Messenger of God (ﷺ), filled all of the human needs and social desires of Abu Dharr. Islam, based in monotheism, opened the gate of struggle, one side of which is God, equality, religion, bread, love, and power, and, on the other side, the arrogance, despotism, discrimination, infidelity (*kufr*), and hunger and the religion of infidelity to the One God which requires weakness and disgrace. Islam, for the first time, put an end to the fairy-tale like-life of the oppressors who plundered what belonged to the people. These oppressors had made the slogan of "to want either this world or the next," the faith of the people, so that "the next world" would be for the people and "this world" for themselves, and, in this way, they gave divine sanctity to poverty.

In this inhuman perception, Islam brought a real revolution into being which said, "Whoever does not have a livelihood will not be saved ... Divine grace, great wealth for society, goodnesses and virtue are part of material life and having bread underlies worshipping God." Monotheism as preached by Allah's Messenger was inseparable from its support for the unity of races, unity of classes, and equity—every person according to his share and right.

It was because of this that Abu Dharr denied himself any material personal life and passed through his own liberation. This liberation, in turn, called for revolutionary devotion and this is also called Islamic austerity. This is necessary if all people are to be provided with materiality and economic equality.

Abu Dharr could be found under the covered Porch (*saffah*) in the corner of the mosque at the height of his success. He had become one of the most intimate friends of the Messenger of God (ص). Whenever he was not in a group, the Prophet asked for him; whenever he was in the group, he turned to him in the midst of speaking.

Under the leadership of the Prophet, in the Battle of Tabuk, when the soldiers with difficulty had to pass through the burning northern desert to reach the borders of eastern Rome, Abu Dharr fell behind. His skinny camel stopped. He freed the camel under the rain of the heat of the desert and set off alone! He found some water. He did not drink of it himself, but took it to give it to his "friend," the Prophet, who was also, undoubtedly, suffering from thirst in such a hot desert.

The Messenger and his companions saw an unclear point moving forward in the distance of the fiery desert. Little by little they sensed that it was a human being. Who was it? Walking and in such a flaming desert, alone at that?

The Messenger, with an ardency overflowing with desire, cried out, "Would that it be Abu Dharr?"

An hour passed. It was Abu Dharr. When he reached the *mu-jahids*, he fell from thirst and exhaustion.

"You are carrying water and you are thirsty, Abu Dharr?" the Messenger asked.

"I thought, in such a hot desert and under such a flaming sun, that you..." Abu Dharr replied.

"May God bless Abu Dharr! He walks alone, dies alone, and will be resurrected alone!" the Messenger of God (ص) said.

IDENTIFICATIONS:

* Jundub ibn Junadah

*Arqam ibn Arqam

CONSIDER AND DISCUSS:

1. How does the verse, "*God charges no soul save to its capacity,*" (2:286) reflect Abu Dharr's state at the moment he chose to cry out against the idols in the Kabah?

2. What does Abu Dharr mean when he says to Mu'awiyyah, "Oh Mu'awiyyah! If you are building your palace with your own money, it is extravagance and if with the money of the people, it is treason?"

BARAKAH:
One Who Nurtures
the Messenger of God (ص)

It was CE 611 or 612. Islam was hidden in the house of Arqam ibn Abi Arqam on the hill of Safa in Makkah. This house was the whole world of Islam and the *ummah* was now perhaps twenty people. Barakah was one of them. Born of Abyssinian parents, she was sold into slavery in Makkah like so many whose names we do not even know. As her name Barakah indicates, she was among the most blessed because she was bought and freed by Abdullah ibn Abu Muttalib and taken to his home to help his wife, Aminah. She was to become one of the women who raised God's Messenger.

Forty years had passed since her days of being a slave. The child she had cared for as a youth was now married and had received the Divine revelation yet he was still a nameless, placeless stranger among the wealthy Quraysh. She had been told by strangers that they had come to the city looking for him and yet had heard nothing but abuse, ridicule, aversion, and hatred about this man, the man she helped raise, the man whom God had chosen as His Messenger. Every place she went in the bazaar she and any strangers who had just arrived in Makkah heard 'respectable people' speak this way, the big shots of religion and the world. They said he was crazy or that he was a magician. With the force of preserving their own economic interests, these people said, "It is not revelation this man speaks, but magic; it is not truth, it is but poetry; he does not receive these words from Gabriel nor are they his own. The truth is, foreign religious scholars —Christian, Jew, or Zoroastrian—dictate the words to him. He is a disgrace to his noble, respected family. He throws the honor of our Temple of Idols—[previously the House of God built by Abraham]—to the winds. He threatens the sacredness of the house of the gods, the tradition of pilgrimage to the idols, and even the daily worship of the gods. He has no respect for the genuineness of his ancestors."

Barakah could not believe what she heard. "How can they be speaking about Muhammad (ﷺ) whom I raised, nurtured, and cared for? This is not he to whom they refer. I know him to be other than this."

She had heard even worse things. Once a man, Unays ibn Junadah, had been looking for Muhammad (ﷺ). He was not having much luck when suddenly he saw a large crowd of people almost tying themselves into knots trying to get to a man alone, with an enlightened face, with a look that aroused the depths of his soul. The man had an open and clear brow and was of middle-size stature. Inspired with kindness and affection, he spoke words more beautiful than poetry, full of fear and hope. Unays did not know whether to listen to the words, give his heart over to the man's charisma, or simply observe the beauty and kindness of his stature, behavior, and words.

He had not reflected upon this for long when a group of angry people appeared. Without listening to the words of the kind and gentle man or even questioning him, they moved right up close to his face and let forth with a flood of abuses and oft-repeated, re-iterated, pre-fabricated insults. With the ignorance that comes from a rule of tyranny and oppression, this group—and many others like them—had nothing that they could lose in the illumination of this man's message and the revolution of this man's mission. They themselves had already been condemned by the ruling system as being 'unimportant' and 'not worth bothering about.' They had been sacrificed to maintain 'things the way they are,' the status quo. The popular masses, with an ugly enthusiasm, shouted out things put into their mouths by those who opposed the Prophet because of their own self-interests.

Barakah knew that it did not matter at all to the Messenger whether the people pushed him away in anger or rage or withdrew from him continuing their abuse and ridicule. He would simply hurry on to another place and amidst another group, begin again and once again, without even being heard, without having been understood, once again he would be attacked with abusive language and accusations, insults, and ridicule and again to another place and again the beginning of what he had to say.

Every time Barakah encountered another story like this, the more firm became her belief and her faith. She was now on her way to the house of Arqam to deliver an important message to the Messenger of God from his beloved wife, Khadijah.

As she moved through the streets of Makkah, heavy with the burden of the message she was bearing, she recalled forty odd years before when she had been helping the Messenger's mother. Aminah had been pregnant and alone. Barakah reminded herself that it had been the Year of the Elephant (CE 570) when the ruler Abraha, the Abyssinian governor in the Yemen, had come with an army to capture Makkah, riding elephants that no one had even seen before.

Abd al-Muttalib, Aminah's father-in-law, was the ruler of Makkah then. He went to see Abraha. When Abraha saw him, he was so impressed by his appearance that he arose from his royal seat to greet him. He ordered his interpreter to find out if Abd al-Muttalib had come to ask a favor. Abd al-Muttalib replied that Abraha's army had taken 200 of his camels and he asked that they should be returned to him. Abraha was surprised. He said that he was disappointed in Abd al-Muttalib because, according to Abraha, Abd al-Muttalib should be concerned with his belief system that Abraha had come to destroy rather than thinking about his own camels. Abd al-Muttalib replied, "I am the lord of the camels and the Kabah likewise has a Lord who will defend it."

Barakah remembered that this happened in the year when Muhammad (ﷺ) had come into the world. Later The Elephant Surah was revealed about this event: *"See you not how your Lord dealt with the Companions of the Elephant? Did He not make their treacherous plan go astray? And He sent against them flights of birds, striking them with stones of baked clay. Then did He make them like an empty field of stalks and straw (of which the corn) has been eaten up"* (105:1-5).

As she hurried along to Arqam's home, Barakah recalled the time when the people of Makkah had rebuilt the Kabah. They were about to lay the Black Stone in place when an argument broke out among the four representatives of the main tribes. Each wanted to himself, on behalf of his tribe, lay the Black Stone (*hajar al-aswad*) in place. An old man had been watching this. In order to end their dispute, he suggested they ask the next person who came into the Kabah area to do it so that they would not have to fight among themselves for this honor. They agreed and the next person who came into the area had been Muhammad (ﷺ), then a young man. They asked him for his help and he gladly gave it. Each one of the four representatives took one corner of the cloth to lift up the stone and Muhammad (ﷺ) laid it in place.

Barakah remembered her own life and the marriage that her beloveds Khadijah and Muhammad (ﷺ) had arranged for her with Ubayd ibn Zayd from the Khazraj tribe of Madinah (Yathrib). She gave birth to a son they named Ayman and so she became known as Umm Ayman, the mother of Ayman. She recalled her husband with good feelings, remembering how he had died soon after that and how she had to raise her son alone.

And now the other 'son' she had raised has been chosen by God as His Messenger. How strange things work—how wise is the Creator. As Barakah approached the house of Arqam, she saw that the idol worshipping Quraysh had blocked off the roads leading there. She had to use great cunning to pass through without them catching her. She did this knowing the fate of getting caught, but that fear weighed nothing in comparison to the trust she had been given to deliver this message. When she gave the message to the Messenger, he smiled and said to her, "You are blessed Umm Ayman. Surely you have a place in Paradise."

After she left to return back to Khadijah, the Messenger turned to his companions and said, "Should any one of you desire to marry a woman from the people of Paradise, let him marry Umm Ayman."

There were a few moments of silence. Umm Ayman was neither beautiful nor attractive. She was by now fifty years old and looked frail. Zayd ibn Haritha, the Messenger's adopted son, came forward and said, "Messenger of God, I will marry Umm Ayman. By God she is better than women who have much grace and beauty."

From their marriage, a son was born, Usamah ibn Zayd Haritha, who was, along with his half-brother, Ayman, to become a companion of the Messenger of God (ﷺ). Umm Ayman migrated to Madinah after the Messenger's migration. She devoted herself to the Muslim cause there just as she had in Makkah. At the Battle of Uhud, she distributed water to the thirsty and saw to the wounds of those wounded in battle. She went with the Messenger's expedition to Khaybar and Hunayn. Her son, Ayman, was martyred in the Battle of Hunayn. Her husband, Zayd, was martyred in the Battle of Mu'tah in Syria.

When the Messenger went with Abu Bakr and Umar to visit her, he asked, "Oh Ummi! Are you well?"

And she replied, "I am well, oh Messenger of God, as long as Islam is well."

After the Messenger died, may God bless him and grant him peace, Barakah often fell into tears. When asked why, she replied "By God, I knew the Messenger of God would die one day. I cry because revelation has come to an end for us."

Umm Ayman died during the caliphate of Uthman. She was among those blessed Muslims about whom the Messenger had said, "It does not matter how you are born (whether you be born a believer or not). What is important is how you die." Umm Ayman, the companion and nurturer of the Messenger of God (ﷺ) died with her place in Paradise assured because of the life of piety and self-sacrifice that she had led.

IDENTIFICATIONS:
* Umm Ayman
* Zayd ibn Haritha
* Abraha
CONSIDER AND DISCUSS:
1. Discuss the laying in place of the Black Stone.
2. Discuss the attempted attack on Makkah by Abraha.

ABDULLAH IBN MAS'UD:
The Teacher

Ibn Mas'ud was to become one of the great reciters of the Quran and he was the founder of the Kufah school of Traditions. Nicknamed Ibn Umm al-Abd ('son of the mother of a slave') and best known in history as Ibn Mas'ud, he began his youth as a shepherd, tending the herd of Uqbah ibn Muayt. He spent his time in the hills around Makkah far from the city and its idolatrous influence. One evening when he returned to Makkah with his flock, he heard the news of a Messenger who had come and who talked of the One God.

Then one day as he was tending Uqbah's flock, he saw two people approaching him from a distance who appeared to be in a hurry. He was surprised to find anyone in this wilderness and two people in a hurry, at that. Who could they be? What could they want? As they came close, he saw that they were tired and thirsty. They greeted him and asked him to milk one of the animals so that they might have something to drink to quench their thirst. Their lips were parched and they spoke with difficulty.

Ibn Mas'ud, the young shepherd, replied to the two men, the Messenger of God and Abu Bakr, although he knew not who they were, "I cannot do that because I do not own these sheep. I am only their caretaker." The two men seeking the retreat of the mountains for a day away from the idol worshipping Quraysh were pleased with his response, so pleased that they did not pursue it although they were thirsty. Ibn Mas'ud was impressed by the fact that they did not insist although he could see their great need. It was not long after that that he converted to Islam.

Ibn Mas'ud offered himself to the service of the Messenger and stopped tending sheep. He accompanied him on his travels and in his battles. He woke him when he was asleep and shielded him when he was bathing. He carried his staff and toothbrush (*siwak*) and saw to his every need.

Being continuously with the Messenger, Ibn Mas'ud learned the *sunnah* of the Prophet from his blessed person. He learned to practice Islam from the person who was the noblest and most perfect model of Islam. Ibn Mas'ud, then, became one of the best known scholars of early Islam and transmitter of Traditions.

Traditions consist of the words the Messenger spoke, the laws he brought, his conduct in relation to the deeds that he performed as well as things about which he remained silent or things with which he did not disagree and deeds he actually performed in his lifetime without telling others that they should perform them. The Traditions are, in short, the Messenger's words and his conduct.

These have been divided into two types: signed rules or rules that existed before Islam and which were confirmed by the Messenger and created rules, rules that had not previously existed which Islam established. Out of these is implied a third which Ibn Mas'ud is able to intuit because of his closeness to the Messenger and that is that the Messenger of God (ص) preserves the form of a rule or the container that has deep roots in society, one to which people have grown accustomed from generation to generation and one that is practiced almost naturally by the people, but he changes the contained, the spirit, direction, and practical application of the rule in a revolutionary and decisive way.

Ibn Mas'ud, this clan-less shepherd, learned this from the Messenger. He saw that the Messenger maintained the "container" of a social custom while inwardly changing the "contained," the "contents." He saw the Messenger taking the rite of the pilgrimage as practiced by the tribes of the idol worshippers and transforming it into a custom for the worship of the One God that was completely contrary to its present usage. The result was that the early converts to Islam did not experience anguish or a new cultural form by going back to the time of Abraham. There was no sense of a loss of positive values, no loss of their customs, but rather they sensed a 'revival,' a 'cleansing' of things that they had considered to be eternal. They could move easily from idolatry to the worship of the One God whereas, in fact, centuries separated them one from the other. The society was not even aware of having left the recent past behind and destroyed the very foundations of idolatry. Ibn Mas'ud was intuitively aware of this leap, this social approach found within the Traditions of the Messenger of God (ص). It is a revolution whereby the container remained permanent while the content changed.

Ibn Mas'ud faced no difficulty in following through with this. One day some of the early converts to Islam were sitting together in Makkah. Ibn Mas'ud was among them. Someone suggested that perhaps the Quraysh leaders were reluctant to accept Islam because they had not heard the recitation of the Quran. "If only someone would recite it for them, perhaps they would understand the truth in the revealed verses," one of them suggested.

Ibn Mas'ud volunteered, "I will recite it for them." The men in the group discouraged him from doing this because he had no clan that would protect him if the Quraysh did anything to him. He insisted, saying, "God will protect me and keep me from harm." He then went to the Kabah and stood where Abraham had stood to rebuild the Kabah with his son, Ishmael. He recited, *"In the Name of God, the Merciful, the Compassionate. The Merciful. He has taught the Quran. He has created the human being and taught him the clear truth"* (55:1-4). By Ibn Mas'ud offering to recite the.Quran for the Quraysh in the Kabah area while standing where Abraham had stood, he showed that he had accepted the place, the "container," but changed the "contents." Now the "contents" were directed towards the worship of the One God. However, only Divine Guidance could inspire them to understand.

Ibn Mas'ud had attracted the attention of the Quraysh. They turned to each other asking what this Ibn Umm Abd, this son of the mother of a slave, was saying.

"Curses be upon him. He is reciting something Muhammad has taught him."

They attacked him and began beating him up. His face bleeding, he returned to the Muslims. "This is what we were afraid would happen," they said. Ibn Mas'ud replied, "I will do the same thing tomorrow if you wish."

They all said, "You have done enough. You have made them hear what they have tried to avoid hearing."

Ibn Mas'ud was also among those cited as a source for some details on the Messenger's nocturnal ascension (*mi'raj*) and on his miraculous journey to Jerusalem (*isra'*). The Quran says, *"Glory to (God) Who took His servant for a journey by night from the Sacred Mosque (Masjid al-Haram) to the Farthest Mosque (Masjid al-Aqsa), whose precincts We did bless—in order that We might show him some of Our Signs for He is All-hearing, All-seeing"* (17:1).

Ibn Mas'ud heard of the Messenger's ascent (*mi'raj*). He learned that the Messenger had been invited to spend the night at the home of the daughter of Abu Talib and Fatimah bint Asad whose name was Umm Hani. She was the sister of Aqil, Ali, and Ja'far. Although her husband had not accepted the Message of God, he always welcomed the Messenger to his home and this time was no exception.

Whenever the Muslims gathered in Umm Hani's house, they would all pray together. One night after they had prayed the night ritual prayer behind the leadership of the Messenger, Umm Hani invited him to spend the night. He accepted but after a brief sleep, he arose and went to the mosque because he especially loved to visit the Kabah during the silent hours of night. While there, the urge for sleep overcame him and he went inside the *hijr* of Ishmael (a semi-circular short wall outside one side of the Kabah) and fell asleep.

He later said, relating the incident, "While I was asleep there, Gabriel came to me and touched me with his foot whereupon I sat upright. I saw nothing and once again lay down. He came a second and a third time. Then he took me by my arm and led me out of the mosque's gate. There was a white animal named Buraq that had wings at his sides by which he moved his legs. Every stride it took was as far as the eye could see.

Ibn Mas'ud transmitted a Tradition of the Messenger as to what happened next: Gabriel accompanied the Messenger who was riding Buraq. They went to Jerusalem. There he found Abraham, the friend of God, Moses, and Jesus (ε) and he prayed with them. Then he was brought three vessels containing milk, wine, and water. A voice said, "If he takes the water, he will be drowned and his people also. If he takes the wine, he will go astray and his people also. If he takes the milk, he will be rightly guided and his people also." Then the Messenger took the vessel of milk and drank it. Gabriel said to him, "You have been rightly guided and so will your people be, Muhammad."

Ibn Mas'ud had heard that the Messenger, led by Gabriel, ascended beyond time and space as riding Buraq, he passed through the seven heavens. The final place of his ascent was the Lote Tree of the Uttermost End as the Quran refers to it. Tabari, one of the earliest commentators upon the Quran, quoted from the Messenger who said, "The Lote Tree is rooted in the Throne and it marks the end of knowledge (*irfan*) of every knower (*arif*), be he the Archangel or Prophet-Messenger. All beyond is a hidden mystery, unknown to any except God alone." And the Quran says, "*Behold the Lote-Tree (sidr) was shrouded in mystery unspeakable, (His) sight never swerved nor did it go wrong! For truly did he see of the Signs of his Lord, the greater*" (53:16-18). The commentators say that the Divine Light descended upon the Lote-Tree and enshrouded it and all else beside. The eye of the Messenger beheld it without wavering and without turning aside from it.

Ibn Mas'ud lived until the time of Caliph Uthman. When he was near death, Caliph Uthman came to see him and asked, "What is your sickness?"

Ibn Mas'ud responded, "My sins."

"What do you need?" the caliph asked.

"The Mercy of my Lord," he responded.

"Shall I give you your wages from the public treasury now?"

"I have no need of it," Ibn Mas'ud responded.

The caliph asked if he did not want it for his children. Ibn Mas'ud replied, "Do you fear poverty for my children? Don't. I have taught them to read The Inevitable Event (*waqi'ah*) Surah every night because I heard the Messenger say, 'Whoever reads The Inevitable Event Surah (56) every night shall not be afflicted with poverty ever.' " Ibn Mas'ud died that night with the remembrance of His Creator on his lips and the recitation of the Holy Quran.

IDENTIFICATIONS:

*** Umm al-Abd**

*** Abraham**

CONSIDER AND DISCUSS:

1. What does it mean to say that the Messenger keeps the container of a ritual, but changes the contained?

2. Discuss the Messenger's *mi'raj*.

SUMAYYAH BINT KHUBBAT:
The First Martyr in Islam

Sumayyah bint Khubbat was the first martyr in Islam. She died from the torture that Abu Jahl inflicted upon her in order to try to get her to renounce her faith and belief that God is One. Abu Jahl was among the most persistent persecutors of Muslims in early Islam. If the converts to Islam came from a powerful tribe that would defend them, Abu Jahl would insult them, mock them, and promise to ruin their reputation. If the converts were merchants, he would threaten to stop their trade by organizing economic sanctions against them; and if the converts were weak and unprotected by a clan, as were Sumayyah, her husband, Yasir, and their son, Ammar, Abu Jahl would torture them and even instigated his powerful allies in many other clans to do the same thing with their weak and unprotected. One day the Messenger passed by and saw Abu Jahl had exposed Sumayyah, Yasir, and Ammar to the heat of the sun. The Messenger said, "Patience, oh family of Yasir. Your meeting-place will be Paradise."

Sumayyah was perhaps aware of the ideas contained in The Constellations Surah (*buruj*) as she accepted Islam. There God swears an oath by three things: the twelve zodiacal signs or *buruj* from which Surah 85 takes its name, by the Day of Judgment when all evil will be punished, and by one who will witness and the person witnessed on that day. The witnesses may be the Prophets, God Himself, and the recording angels along with the sinner's own misused limbs and record of deeds. Just as surely as these things exist like the constellations or will come to pass like the Day of Judgment and witnesses and witnessed, so shall those who persecute the believers be punished in hell fire for what they do.

"Behold! They sat over against the (fire) and they witnessed (all) that they were doing against the believers. And they ill-treated (the believers) for no other reason than that they believed in God, exalted in power, worthy of praise—He to Whom belongs the dominion of the heavens and the earth! And God is Witness to all things. Those who persecute the believers, men and women, and do not turn in repentance will have the penalty of hell: they will have the penalty of the burning fire" (85:6-10). And Sumayyah knew, *"For those who believe and do righteous deeds will be Gardens beneath which rivers flow: that is the great Salvation"* (85:11).

And the Quran says, *"As to those who deny the Signs of God, and, in defiance of right, slay the Prophets and slay those who teach just dealing with mankind, announce to them a grievous penalty"* (3:21). Perhaps Sumayyah understood the social implications pervading the philosophy of humanity's history. Perhaps she could place the Signs of God, the Prophets, and those people like herself who call others to equality on one side and those who cover over the truth (*kuffar*) of God, those who slay the Prophets, and those who slay people who seek justice on the opposite side.

She knew that the Messenger of God was the last Messenger.

He and all those who preceded him had come to teach the world wisdom, the Book, and justice. Prophet Muhammad (ﷺ) had come to bring unity to races, to groups, to families, and to social classes in order to destroy the discord that had arisen among them by the concerted efforts of those who worship other than the One God and in order to supplant this with the world view of monotheism (*tawhid*). The slogan of unity that Sumayyah knew and in which she believed with all her heart to the point that she was willing to die for this principle is a liberating slogan. It is because of this freedom and liberation from all that divides humankind and a movement towards all that unites, that a special sensitivity to monotheism developed among the slaves, the whipped, the hungry, and the oppressed of history, the morale of whom was weakened by people like Abu Jahl who only thought about his own economic interests and of preserving the status quo.

This was why the group of early converts that Sumayyah joined, those who gathered around the Messenger of God in Makkah were, for the most part, among the most deprived, the most forgotten of the scorned. This was why Sumayyah heard the enemies of Islam refer to her 'kind' as 'too poor to make a difference'.

Sumayyah sensed something else. She sensed that this was the greatest praise that could be given to Islam. Islam changed values of self-interest into values for humankind as a whole. She saw the Messenger of God as a savior for the slaves who were certain that their only fate was slavery. Slaves or the scorned and despised, for they are one and the same, heard the language of coercion of Abu Jahl, that only he and his interests should be served. They were treated in a way to believe that they were only born to experience suffering, to bear hardship, and the heavy loads that others above them are unwilling to carry and—to go hungry. This class of the deprived to which Sumayyah belonged in early Islam—were convinced by a system of multitheism that they were created by the gods to work for their creators just as the founder of Manichaeism, had said many years before the birth of Sumayyah — "The wretched and deprived are of the essence of darkness and the powerful conquerors are of the essence of light." Even Plato and Aristotle, founders of the intellectual thought of Western civilization, said, "God or nature creates one group as slaves and another group, free, so that the free can attend to higher affairs such as morals, art, poetry, music, and civilization. They are able to do this because of the toil and suffering which the deprived undertake in lowly and abased tasks."

Sumayyah knew the Messenger of God had begun a different kind of movement, a movement in opposition to deception, falsehood, multitheism, discord, a sense of superiority, and class differences. He announced that all of humanity was of one race, from one source, and had one God. He declared equality for all and followed this.

He destroyed all values that had taken the form of idols and shattered all values of ignorance and the aristocratic way of thinking, much as his ancestor, Abraham, had done. He commanded his followers to take the scissors to the long, splendid robes some of them wore. He ordered them to chop off their long beards that was a sign of aristocracy in early Islam. He ordered people not to walk in arrogance and hautiness down the streets and narrow passage ways. He instructed people to ride two at a time upon a horse. And, in order to break down aristocratic values, he sometimes even rode bareback upon a donkey.

Sumayyah knew that the Messenger of God was from among themselves. *"It is He Who has sent amongst the unlettered (umiiyun) a Messenger from among themselves, to rehearse to them His Signs, to sanctify and to instruct them in the Book and Wisdom, although they had been before that in clear error"* (62:2). The emphasis is on the fact that the Prophets are from among the people as were all of the Abrahamic Prophets. They were human beings from among the people (*nas*), not from the select, noble, elite, and selective classes of society as Abu Jahl and his followers considered themselves to be because of their economic circumstances. The Messenger of God, "*...spoke in the language of his people...*" (14:4) which means he spoke to them in a way that related to their needs and not as a philosopher, poet, or scholar who spoke in a way that someone like Sumayyah would not understand. The Messenger of God spoke directly to those things which caused the deprived anguish. This was the way of the Abrahamic Prophets—to struggle for the masses of the people against the existing power of the time which rules over the people in the name of other than the One God.

Sumayyah sensed, as she bore the torture of being chained in place to die from the heat of the hot Makkan sun, that the Messenger of God (ﷺ) brought the same message that Abraham, Moses, Jesus (ﷺ), and other Prophets had brought. Their message, however, had been forgotten and buried with the passage of time. What they had all said was "submit to the Will of God" (*islam*) in opposition to those who would surrender to the will of themselves and everything other than God. She felt that he had stood up to save her and all those who were rightly guided from powerful, aristocrats like Abu Jahl. The Messenger of God explained that just as there is One God, so there is one way, one religion, one spirit, one class—the believers— and but one slogan: "There is no deity but God and Muhammad is the Messenger of God." Sumayyah died under the torture of Abu Jahl with these words upon her lips. This first martyr in Islam—and a woman at that—through her martyrdom kept the movement of Islam alive. We know for sure not to say, "*...of those who are slain in the Way of God: 'They are dead.' Nay, they are living...though we perceive not*" (2:154). *And again, "Think not of those who are slain in God's Way as dead. Nay, they live, finding their sustenance in the Presence of their Lord"* (3:169).

IDENTIFICATIONS:
* Ammar Yasir
* Abu Jahl
* Abrahamic Prophets
CONSIDER AND DISCUSS:
1. Discuss the meaning of the verse, "...spoke in the language of his people..." (14:4).
2. What social ills result from a system where other than the One God is worshiped?

BILAL IBN RABAH:
The First Caller to Ritual Prayer

Bilal ibn Rabah, sometimes called Ibn Hamana after his mother, was one of the first companions to accept Islam from the Messenger of God (ﷺ), a decision for which he paid heavily. Later known as having been the *mu'adhdhin* or "caller to ritual prayer," Bilal was born into slavery in Makkah, being the slave of Umayyah ibn Khalaf. Umayyah ibn Khalaf was a cruel tyrant and an enemy of Islam until his death. When Umayyah heard of Bilal's conversion to Islam, he thought that he would be able to make him change his mind if he tortured him. His arrogance would not allow him to accept the idea that his slave could adopt the faith of Muhammad.

Had not Bilal seen the Messenger of God wandering the streets of Makkah looking for crowds of people to whom to tell his message? He saw the Prophet standing before the people and, without thinking about what they may say, tried to help them fear

God, gave them tidings of the Day of Judgment, warned them of the dangers of not heeding, showed them the way to salvation for he had a Message. His Message was from the One Who befriends the honorable and the One Who was an enemy of the arrogant (*mustakbir*) for it had been revealed to him, "*Oh you wrapped up (in a mantle)! Arise and deliver your warning*" (74:1-2).

The Messenger had been told to warn those who are asleep, who slumbered in the tranquillity of their ignorance and the security of their tyranny and arrogance as those who rebel against God's commands (*taghut*). These were people who shepherd the wolf within while grazing the people/sheep without on humiliation. The One God whose message had been given to Abraham, Moses, Jesus, and His last Messenger, Muhammad (ص) is the One God Who commanded the angels to bow down before His creation of humankind. And now, in the Makkah of Arabia in the early seventh century, descendants of Adam were being required by the multitheists to bow down before the feet of those who follow satan—the carvers, and guardians of whom were the supporters of classes and clans.

Bilal, the slave of Ethiopian descent, did not fit into their picture, into their class, and as he had no protecting clan, he was among those most severely tortured. The Quraysh showed special enmity towards this group of the slaves and the deprived. They imprisoned them, beat them, denied them food or drink, and exposed them to the heat of the sun in order to get them to renounce their faith. And Umayyah ibn Khalaf devised unheard of tortures towards breaking Bilal's resistance. He dressed him in a suit of armor and made him lie in the hot mid-day sun until the metal scorched his skin. When this failed, he put heavy stones, hot from the heat of the sun, on his chest. Bilal was then asked if he believed in the idols Lat and Uzza. Bilal, under the strain of the heat and the heavy stone burning through his skin, repeated over and over again, "*Say: God is One; Say: God is One...*" (112:1) The

Quraysh were amazed by his ability to resist the merciless brutality. Even Umayyah was beginning to think that he would have to use a new tactic because this one was not working.

The Messenger of God (ﷺ) walked by and saw Bilal being tortured. He found Abu Bakr and asked him to buy Bilal's freedom which Abu Bakr did by saying to Umayyah, "Are you going to kill this slave for nothing? Why don't you sell him to me?"

Umayyah thought for a few moments and then said, "I will be glad to be rid of him, but I want a good price for him."

Abu Bakr replied, "Of course. I will pay your price."

Upon hearing that the transaction had been completed, the Prophet thanked Abu Bakr for his deed.

Once the Messenger of God had migrated to Madinah and the efforts of the emigrants (*muhajirun*) and helpers (*ansar*) were arranged, Islam became firmly established. Ritual prayer (*salat*) was instituted along with the tax known as the poor-rate (*zakat*). Fasting during the month of Ramadan was made obligatory and Islam took its place among *"those who...had homes (in Madinah) and had adopted the faith—and who show their affection to those who came to them for refuge and entertain no desire in their hearts for things given (by them) to (the emigrants) but give them preference over themselves, even though poverty is their own lot and those saved from the covetousness of their own souls—they are the ones that achieve prosperity"* (59:9).

The people gathered around him at the appointed time of the ritual prayer without there being a call to prayer. The Messenger of God considered using a trumpet like the Jews did to call the people to prayer. He disregarded this idea and ordered a wooden clapper (*naqus*) to be used.

Then one night Abdullah ibn Zayd, a man from the Khazraj tribe, had a dream that he recounted to the Messenger the next day. He said, "In my dream, a man wearing two green garments passed by me and he carried a wooden clapper in his hands. I said to him, 'Oh slave of God, will you sell the wooden clapper to me?'

"He asked, 'What will you do with it?'

"I responded, 'We will call the people to ritual prayer with it.'

"Then he asked, 'Shall I not show you a better way?'

"'What way is that?' I asked anxiously.

"He answered, 'You should say: "God is Greater (*Allah akbar*).' The man in green repeated this glorification of God four times and then each of the following twice: 'I bear witness that there is no deity but God; I testify that Muhammad is the Messenger of God; come unto the prayer; come unto salvation; God is Greater' and then once again, 'there is no deity but God.'"

The Messenger of God confirmed that Abdullah ibn Zayd had had been inspired. He told him to go to Bilal, who had a beautiful voice, and teach him exactly the words expressed to him in the dream. In this way, Bilal became the first "caller to ritual prayer" in Islam.

A woman from the Najjar tribe who lived near the mosque said to Bilal, "My house is among the highest that surround the mosque. Use it to call people to ritual prayer." Bilal, then, everyday before dawn went to her rooftop to await the time for the dawn (*fajr*) prayer. When he saw the first light of dawn, he stretched out his arms and said in prayer, "Oh God, I praise You and I ask Your Help for the Quraysh, that they may accept Your religion." Then he stood and called the people to ritual prayer.

Bilal became one of the closest Companions of the Holy Prophet. He accompanied him everywhere. His high-pitched, resonant voice as he called people to ritual prayer had a particular hypnotic quality to it that drew people more readily to the ritual prayer.

At the Battle of Badr, after the Messenger's migration to Madinah, Bilal challenged his cruel master, Ibn Khalaf, and succeeded in killing him. When Abu Bakr learned of this, he said, "Oh Bilal, how sweet is divine justice."

When Makkah fell, Bilal entered the area of the Kabah alongside the Messenger who told him to go on top of the Kabah and recite the call to ritual prayer. Bilal obeyed and saw the entire valley was echoing the hypnotic sounds of Bilal's voice. People rushed to form their ranks for the first ritual prayer after the conquest of Makkah and near the Kabah, at that, the place from whence they had been obliged to flee.

When the Messenger was leaving the Battle of Khaybar, towards the end of the night, he asked, "Who will watch over us until dawn so that we may sleep?" Bilal volunteered. Bilal prayed as long as he could. He propped himself up against his camel and just as he was looking at the rising of the dawn, he fell asleep. The others awoke soon after that feeling the heat of the rising sun.

The Messenger went a short distance away, made his camel kneel. He and the men performed the ablutions. He ordered Bilal to give the call to ritual prayer. Then the Messenger led them in prayer. Having finished, he went to them and said, "If you forget your ritual prayers, perform them when you remember them for God has said, *'Perform ritual prayer for My remembrance'*" (20:14).

One day the Messenger was sitting in the Mosque in Madinah. Abd al-Rahman went to him and said, "Messenger of God! My sister is of marriageable age. Please suggest a suitable match."

The Messenger said, "What about Bilal?" The young man heard but did not respond.

A few days later he returned and asked the same question and again the Messenger replied, "What about Bilal?"

The young man, again, went away and, again, a few days later returned with the same question but this time when the Messenger replied, "What about Bilal?" Abd al-Rahman responded, saying, "Messenger of God, my sister will be most happy to be the wife of a man you hold in such regard."

Bilal was known for his piety and sincerity in whatever he did and humility in all situations that won him great esteem in the heart of his Muslim brothers. Whenever someone would praise him while he was present, he would respond by saying, "I am only a Black man who until yesterday was a slave." May God rest his soul in peace.

IDENTIFICATIONS:

* taghut

* salat

* zakat

CONSIDER AND DISCUSS:

1. Discuss how the "call to prayer" developed.

2. How does the Quran describe the emigrants?

KHABBAB AL-ARATT:
The Blacksmith

Khabbab, an Arab sold into slavery as a result of a raid against his clan of the Banu Tamim, was among the early companions of God's Messenger. He suffered great torture at the hands of his owner, Umm Anmar. A blacksmith by trade, Khabbab had seen the Messenger of God being insulted, conspired against, threatened, and ridiculed in an attempt by the aristocratic Quraysh to try to silence him, make him 'not speak,' and yet he spoke. Khabbab understood from his message the idea in the verse, *"And We wished to be gracious to those that were deprived upon the earth and to make them leaders ('aimah) and to make them the heirs"* (28:3)

He saw that whenever the Messenger was in an assembly, he invited people to God. He recited the Quran for them and warned the Quraysh of what happened to former people. He saw a person from the Abd al-Manaf clan arise after that and address the people about the mythical heroes of Kings, Rustam and Isfandiyar, saying, "By God, Muhammad cannot tell a story better than I.

His talk is of old fables that he has simply repeated in the same way that I repeat them."

The Quran tells of people who say things like this and the response to give them, "*And they say, 'Tales of the ancients which he (Muhammad) has caused to be written; and they are dictated before him morning and evening'. Say: 'The (Quran) was sent down by Him Who knows the mystery (that is) in the heavens and the earth; verily He is Oft-Forgiving, Most Merciful*" (25:5-6).

The Messenger warned them in the words of the Quran, "*Verily you (unbelievers) and the gods that you worship besides Allah are but fuel for hell! To it will you surely come*" (21:98).

And again, the unbelievers are warned, "*Woe to each sinful dealer in falsehood. He hears the Signs of God rehearsed to him, yet he is obstinate and arrogant as if he has not heard them. Then announce to him a penalty grievous. And when he learns something of Our Signs, He takes them in jest. For such there shall be a humiliating penalty*" (45:7-9).

Khabbab was among those who suffered torture in order to preserve their faith in God. His master, Umm Anmar, taught him to be a blacksmith in order to make use of his talents. Before the call to prophethood, Muhammad (ﷺ) used to sit in front of Khabbab's workshop as he had grown very fond of him. Khabbab then accepted Islam once the invitation was given to him by Muhammad (ﷺ). When Umm Anmar heard of his conversion to Islam, she took a hot iron and branded him on his head. Khabbab complained of her actions to the Messenger. The Messenger prayed for him, saying, "Oh Lord, help Khabbab." Umm Anmar developed a very painful illness from which she died.

Khabbab recalled being told that one day the Messenger of God was sitting in the mosque with a group of the Quraysh. The Messenger was interrupted by a Quraysh and then silenced him with his answers. He recited for him and the others, "*Verily you (unbelievers) and the (false) gods that you worship beside God are but fuel for hell. You will come to it. If these had been gods, they would not have come to it, but all will be in it everlastingly. They will be wailing and they will not hear"* (21:98-99).

The Messenger then left and another Quraysh came and sat down. He was told of how Muhammad (ﷺ) had managed to silence one of the Quraysh. The man who had most recently joined the group said, "Ask Muhammad, 'Is everything which is worshiped besides God in hell with those who worship it?' We worship the angels. The Jews worship Uzayr and the Christians worship Jesus, son of Mary." The Quraysh in the assembly were heartened to hear his logic and, to them, convincing argument.

Khabbab heard that when the Messenger of God was told of this, he said, "Everyone who wishes to be worshiped to the exclusion of God shall be with those who worship him. They worship only satans and those they have been ordered to worship." And the verse was revealed, *"Those who have received kindness from us in the past will be removed far from it and will not hear its sound and they abide eternally in their heart's desire"* (21:101). Commentators say, 'heart's desire' refers to Jesus, son of Mary, and Uzayr and those rabbis and monks who have lived in obedience to God, but whom erring people worship as lords beside God.

And it was revealed concerning their assertion that they worship angels and that they are the daughters of God, *"And they say: 'The Merciful has begotten offspring. Glory be to Him. They are but servants raised to honor. They do not speak before he speaks and they carry out His commands. He knows what is before them and what is behind them and they offer no intercession except for those who are acceptable and they stand in awe and reverence of His glory. If any of them should say, 'I am a god besides Him,' such a one We should reward with hell. Thus do We reward those who do wrong"* (21:26-29).

As to those who worship Jesus, Khabbab was clear about where they were. People who worship Jesus are people who reject Jesus' position as a Prophet like other Prophets before him and the Prophet Muhammad (ص) after him. They ridicule him as this because by worshipping him and raising him to the position of a deity, they can justify their own desire to worship many gods and to create many classes among people. The Quran confirms this, *"When (Jesus) the son of Mary is held up as an example, behold your people ridicule this"* (43:57). Then it refers to Jesus, son of Mary, saying, *"He was no more than a servant. We granted Our favor to him and We made him an example of the Children of Israel. And if it were Our Will, We could make angels from amongst you, succeeding each other on the earth. And (Jesus) shall be a Sign (for the coming of) the Hour (of Judgment). Therefore, have no doubt about the (Hour), but follow Me. This is the Straight Way"* (43:57-61).

The unbelievers in Makkah did not leave Khabbab alone either. They put chain mail on him as they did with Bilal and Ammar and then put him in the hot sun so that the chain mail burned through his skin. In spite of all of this torture, not once did Khabbab agree to the terms of the unbelievers and renounce his faith. Sometimes they would light a fire and they would make him stand near the fire until the sweat of his body put the fire out. Sometimes they would take stones baked hot in the sun and lay them on his back until his back burned and pressed into his flesh.

Once Ammar asked him, "What have the unbelievers done to you?"

He said, "If you want to know, look at my back."

When Ammar saw the scars, he was pained for him and said, "I have never seen a back so burned."

The torture inflicted by the unbelievers had not been limited to physical torture. They also harmed the Muslims economically as well as in other ways. Once when Khabbab gave some swords he had made to Aas ibn Wail and asked for payment, he was told, "Does Muhammad not say that those who will go to heaven will have everything that they want there?"

Khabbab said, "Yes. He has said that."

He was then told, "Therefore, have patience. We will pay you on the Day of Judgment from the gold and silver that will be there. I swear that you and your believers are not closer to the gods than I am." These verses were revealed to the Messenger, *"Have you not then seen the (sort of) men who reject Our Signs, yet say: 'I shall certainly be given wealth and children.' Has he penetrated to the Unseen or has he taken a contract with the Merciful? Nay, We shall record what he says and We shall add and add to his punishment. To Us shall return all that he talks of and he shall appear before Us bare and alone. And they have taken (for worship) gods other than God to give them power and glory. Instead, they shall reject their worship and become adversaries against them"* (19:77-82).

Then there was the story of ibn Khalaf who took an old bone to the Prophet that was crumbling to pieces. He asked, "Muhammad, do you allege that God can revive this after it has decayed?" Then he crumbled it even further and blew the dust on the Prophet's face. The Prophet answered, "Yes. I say that God will raise it and you after yours have become like this dust. Then God will send you to hell." And it is revealed in the Quran, *"And he makes comparisons for Us and forgets his own (origin) and creation. He says, 'Who can give life to (dry) bones and decomposed men (at that)?' Say: 'He will give them life Who created them for the first time for He is well-aware in every kind of creation! The same Who produces for you fire out of the green tree, when behold! You kindle therewith (your own fires). Is He Who created the heavens and the earth not able to create the like'? Yea, indeed! For He is the Creator Supreme, of skill and knowledge (infinite). Verily when He intends a thing, His Command is, 'Be,' and it is"* (36:78-83).

And then once when the Messenger was going around the Kabah, he met some of the Quraysh leaders. They said, "Muhammad, come let us worship what you worship and you worship what we worship. You and we will join together in this way. If what you worship is better than what we worship, we will take a share of it and if what we worship is better than what you worship, you can take a share of it." God reveals concerning this, *"Say: oh unbelievers, I do not worship what you worship and you do not worship what I worship. You have your religion and I have mine"* (109). In effect it says, "If you will only worship the One God on condition that I worship what you worship, I have no need of you at all. You can have your religion, all of it, and I have mine."

Khabbab found release from his pain and suffering only after the Messenger gave him permission to migrate to Madinah. Khabbab was generously provided for by the helpers. He was at peace being near the Messenger and as a result of his hard work in Madinah, Khabbab was blessed with great wealth. He was very generous and was said to have allowed those who were in need to take from whatever he had. Yet in spite of his generosity he continued to fear that he might not have done enough for others.

When Khabbab died, the fourth righteous caliph, Caliph Ali, stood at his grave site and said, "God's Mercy be on Khabbab. He freely accepted Islam; he willingly migrated to Madinah; and, he lived as a *mujahid*. God shall not withhold the reward of one who has done good."

IDENTIFICATIONS:
* Ibn Khalaf
* Umm Anmar
CONSIDER AND DISCUSS:
1. What does God promise the deprived?
2. Discuss the Quran's answer to people who worship
angels or Jesus as deities.

UMAR IBN KHATTAB:
The Strong-Willed

Four years before the Messenger's migration to Madinah, Umar ibn al-Khattab, who was then twenty-six years old, accepted Islam. Both his sister, Fatimah and her husband, Sa'id ibn Zayd, had become Muslims but were concealing the fact from their family. Khabbab al-Aratt would often go to Fatimah's house to recite the Quran. One day Umar left his home with his sword unsheathed, heading for the house of Arqam where he heard the Messenger and a number of his companions had gathered—about forty in all, including women. Among the forty were Hamzah, Abu Bakr, and Ali.

One of the recent converts to Islam, who concealed his conversion, saw Umar in his angry state and asked him where he was going. Umar said, "I am going to kill Muhammad, the apostate, who has split the Quraysh, made mockery of their traditions, insulted their faith and their gods."

The man said, "Umar you deceive yourself. Do you think for

one moment that the Abd al-Manaf (Muhammad's protectors) would allow you to continue walking upon the earth when you have killed Muhammad? Would it not be better for you to go and set your own family in order?"

Umar asked, "What is the matter with my family?"

"Your brother-in-law, Sa'id, and your sister, Fatimah, have become Muslims and follow Muhammad. You should talk with them first."

Umar changed his plans and headed for his sister's house. There he found Khabbab al-Aratt reciting the Quran for his sister and brother-in-law. Khabbab was teaching them Surah TaHa. When they heard Umar's voice, Khabbab hid in a small room and Fatimah concealed the verses they were reading under her leg but Umar had heard the recitation of Khabbab as he neared the house. When he came in, he said, "What is all this gibberish I am hearing?"

They said, "You have not heard anything."

"Yes, I have," he insisted, "and I have been told that you follow Muhammad in his religion."

He grabbed hold of his brother-in-law. His sister Fatimah stood up in his defense. He hit Fatimah. When they saw that things were at this point, they said, "Yes, we are Muslim. We believe in the One God and His Prophet. Do whatever you want."

When Umar saw blood on his sister, he felt very ashamed for what he had done. He turned back and said, "Give me what you were reciting so that I may see for myself what Muhammad has brought."

Fatimah replied that she was afraid to trust him with it. "Do not be afraid," he said and he swore that he would give it back to her once he had read it.

Hearing this, her heart filled with hope that perhaps Umar would accept Islam. She said, "My brother, you are impure because of your idolatry and only the pure can touch these words."

Umar stood up and went and washed himself. Then she gave him the page containing the verses from Surah TaHa: *"In the Name of God, the Merciful, the Compassionate. TaHa. We have not sent down the Quran to you to be (an occasion) for your distress, but only as an admonition to those who fear (God)—a revelation from Him Who created the earth and the heavens on high (God) Most Gracious is firmly established on the Throne (of authority). To Him belongs what is in the heavens and on earth, and all between them, and all beneath the soil. If you pronounce the word aloud (it is no matter) for verily He knows what is secret and what is yet more hidden. God! There is no deity but He! To Him belong the Most Beautiful Names"* (20:1-8).

When he had finished reading it, he said, "How fine and noble this is."

Khabbab heard his words and came out saying, "Oh Umar, by God. I hope that God has singled you out by His Prophet's call. Come to God, come to God, oh Umar."

Hearing this, Umar said, "Lead me to Muhammad so that I may accept Islam."

Khabbab responded by saying that he was in the house of Arqam in the Safa hill with a number of his companions.

Umar took his sheathed sword and went to see the Messenger. He knocked at the door. When they heard his voice, one of the companions got up and looked through a crack in the door. He saw he was wearing his sword. He went to the Messenger and told him in fear, "It is Umar and he is wearing his sword."

Hamzah said to the Messenger, "Let him in. If he has ill-intentions, we will kill him with his own sword."

The Messenger said, "Let him in." When Umar came in, he asked him what he wanted.

"Oh Messenger of God, I have come to you to believe in God and His Messenger and what he has brought from God."

The Messenger gave thanks to God so loudly that everyone in the house heard that Umar had become a Muslim. The meeting broke up with the companions feeling confidence in the situation now that both Umar and Hamzah had accepted Islam because they knew that they would protect the Messenger.

Abdullah ibn Umar, the son of Umar and also a companion of the Messenger, related, "When my father became a Muslim, he asked some people, 'Who among the Quraysh is best at spreading rumors?' He was told that it was so and so. He went to him and I followed to see what would happen. Although I was young, I understood everything I saw. He went to the man and asked, 'Do you know that I have become a Muslim?' By God, hardly had the words left his mouth when the man got up, dragging his cloak on the ground, Umar following, and I following my father, Umar. He stood by the door of the mosque and cried out at the top of his voice while the Quraysh were in their meeting places around the Kabah, 'Umar has apostatized.' Umar stood behind him and shouted, 'He is a liar. I have become a Muslim and I bear witness that there is no deity but God and that Muhammad is the Messenger of God.'

"The Quraysh got up and attacked him. The fighting continued for some time. Finally Umar was tired and sat down, saying, 'Do as you will but I swear by God that if we had been three hundred men, we would have fought it out on equal terms.'

"At this point a Shaykh of the Quraysh came forward and asked what was going on. When he was told that Umar had apostatized, he said, 'Why should a man not choose a religion for himself? What are you trying to do? Let the man alone.' By God, it was as though they were a garment stripped off him."

Always ready to protect the Messenger whom he came to love deeply, it is recorded that while in Madinah after the Battle of Badr, Umar ibn Khattab was ready to defend the Messenger against Umayr ibn Wahb Jumahi. History tells us the following:

Umayr ibn Wahb Jumahi was among the outstanding leaders of the Quraysh. He participated in the Battle of Badr on the side of the unbelievers of Makkah against the Muslims. It could even be said that he was one of the ones responsible for fanning the flames of war when they were about to be extinguished and it looked like no battle would take place. Once the Muslims had taken up their battle positions at Badr, he was told to go and see how many Muslims there were and where they were located. Umayr saddled his horse and went to spy on the Muslims. He returned to the Quraysh and said that the Muslims were about three hundred strong or a little more. He then said that the most important news he had was the commitment he noticed in the few soldiers. He pointed out that the Makkans should not become overconfident by the fact that the Muslims were so few in number because he also saw great committment on the part of the Muslim soldiers. He saw they were all prepared to die, if necessary. Thirst would not deter them from their goal of at least killing an equal number of Quraysh before they died.

Just before the Battle of Badr began, Umayr attacked the Muslims, riding amongst their ranks. He threw himself off of his horse so that the Makkan forces would move with fervor to revenge him, thereby entering into the battle in full force. Umayr was saved during the battle, but his son, Wahd, was taken as a prisoner-of-war.

After the Quraysh forces returned to Makkah, Umayr, who was trying to figure out a way to get his son back, was walking near the Kabah when he saw Safwan ibn Umayyah. He sat next to him and they began to speak of their misery. Safwan said to him, "Life is not worth living after the defeat we suffered at Badr and all of the great men that we lost."

Umayr confirmed what Safwan was saying and added, "I swear if I did not have debts and were not concerned about my family's means of support, I would go to Madinah and in the first encounter with Muhammad, I would kill him because I have heard that he walks freely in Madinah without bodyguard or escort. If anyone were to see me and recognize me, I would say that

I have come in regard to my son who is a prisoner."

Safwan became pleased hearing this and said, "Do you really mean it?"

"Yes," Umayr answered, "I swear by the idols of this house that I would do just that."

Safwan said, "If you agree to do this, I will pay your debts and support your family while you are gone like my own family and you know that in Makkah, no one cares more for their family than I do. Rest assured that they will be cared for in comfort."

Safwan prepared the things that Umayr would need for his journey. He mounted him on his own camel and placed a poisoned sword in his hand. Umayr left for Madinah.

Umayr entered Madinah. He dismounted before the Prophet's mosque in Madinah. He hobbled his camel and unsheathed his sword. He moved towards implementing the plan for which he had come. Umar ibn Khattab was sitting with a group inside the mosque. They were speaking about the victory of Badr. The minute Umar's eyes fell on the armed Umayr, he jumped up from his place and cried out, "This is that very enemy of God who at Badr fanned the flames of war and reported to the Quraysh that the Muslims were very few in number." The Muslims in the mosque surrounded Umayr. Umar told the Messenger about him and how they had found him armed. He said, "Oh Messenger of God, Umayr is a dangerous and clever, fearless man. Do not trust him."

"Let him come forward," the Messenger said.

Umayr, still holding his unsheathed sword in his hand, moved forward inside the mosque. The Prophet said, "Umar, let go of him." Umar let him go. After talking to the Messenger, Umayr converted to Islam.

Umar ibn Khattab was a man of strong will. He was to become the second rightly-guided caliph and father-in-law of the Messenger of God (ﷺ) when the Messenger married Umar's daughter, Hafsa. Once he heard the words of the revelation, God guided him towards 'submission to the Will of God' (*islam*) and he spent the rest of his life in support of Islam. He died at the hands of an assassin at the age of fifty-three. May Allah rest his soul in peace.

IDENTIFICATIONS:
 * **Negus**
* **Fatimah bint al-Khattab**
* **Umayr ibn Jumahi**
CONSIDER AND DISCUSS:
1. Discuss Umar's concern for the Messenger after his conversion to Islam.
2. Discuss Umayr ibn Jumahi's treachery which turned into conversion.

UMM DHARR:
She, Too, Dies Alone

One of the earliest women companions of the Messenger of God, Umm Dharr, like her husband Abu Dharr became 'a complete human being' in the school of Islam in spite of having spent a lifetime in the poverty and hardships of rural life. Perhaps there are some who look for the glory of Islam in the victories of its armies and the creation of a great empire—for a time. What is the difference between the Islamic movement and other political and military movements in history which attained the same heights in terms of worldly gains for awhile? What does Islam do? What is attained from all the sacrifices and struggles of the Messenger of God and his God-fearing, pious companions.

Here we are looking at a religion—Islam—which obligates the human being to hold all of creation in trust and in doing so to universally elevate creation, obliging mankind to evolve to higher states of order, to develop, progress, and ascend. Just as God created causes in nature which turn the inanimate into the plant and the plant into an animal and the animal into the human being and each finds its own completion, so religion becomes a cause for the amazing story of creation to continue and to allow the human spirit to reach the highest summit beyond time and place. Religion, then, can be seen as the instigator, stimulant, and impetus behind the human being moving up the ladder of transformation. In this light, religion becomes as a factory in which the real and total human being is built and we should expect nothing less than this from religion.

In order to test this theory we will be looking at the life of Umm Dharr, the wife of Abu Dharr, and companion of the Messenger of God, a person who would have fallen into the cracks of any other history except that of Islam. She would have been considered marginal and, therefore, unworthy of mention.

But Islam does not look at the human being this way. It looks at the nameless masses, oppressed slaves, and the exhausted as models for humanity. No longer is it the aristocracy-worshipping history which prevails in early Islam but the history of the mud-houses of the African slaves, the history of the bare-footed bedouin, and the history and struggles of a poor woman like Umm Dharr. The history of Islam has recorded the deeds of people like her with a sense of pride and joy because it has happened but a handful of times in human history and these few are then offered with honor to the future generations.

Therefore, in order to understand the results attained by the Islamic movement of the Messenger of God, one must not look to the victories in Asia, Africa, and in southern Europe. Rather one must attend to and make note of the movement as it developed in the thoughts, brains, hearts, and souls of a very few number of its followers. The victory that Islam gained in the spirits of these people appears more splendid, more extensive, and more wondrous to those who place greater value on truth and humanness than on power and external military domination.

It is not an exceptional history to be able to point to ancient kings and conquerors like Alexander, Ghengis Khan, and Napoleon. Rather, structuring a nameless, poverty-stricken bedouin like the wife of Jundub ibn Junadah into an Umm Dharr Ghifari is unique in every ideology and in every movement.

Strange changes began to appear in the Ghifar tribe three years before the mission of the Messenger of God is actualized. Like the instinctive scent of wild birds who know when a storm is brewing and hurriedly seek shelter or like the wondrous instinct of horses who arise just before an earthquake comes, tear away the bridle and head for safety, lonely spirits sense that there is something in the air. This is how it is for Umm Dharr and her husband, Abu Dharr.

They are children of a bedouin tribe of the Ghifar, a poverty-stricken tribe from Rabadhah. A wilderness between Makkah and Madinah, Rabadhah is located on the route of the Quraysh caravans and the pilgrims going to the Kabah which is still a place where idols are worshiped. The tribe is known to the bedouins as brazen men and women who are fearless before all customs, rules, and laws. In the eyes of the pagan Quraysh, the Ghifar are notorious, evil, reckless, and morally corrupt. The pagan's view of morality is based on keeping things exclusive for the wealthy who are the 'privileged' class. The basis of this morality is to give the wealthy man, security and peace of mind so that he can eat well and enjoy himself at the head of his sumptuous feasts, turning his back on those who are outside and hungry.

The Quraysh consider the Ghifar to be bandits—bandits who rob the goods and slaves of the commercial caravans and who do not even hold the four sacred months in respect. When these caravans—moving between eastern Rome, Makkah, and Iran—protected by the custom not to fight during four particular months of the year—reach Rabadhah, they suddenly come upon the Ghifar, swords overhead, flying out from their place of ambush against the caravans. These people of Ghifar—'poor, sinful, and wicked,' instead of extending a beggar's bowl to the commercial caravans, offer them their swords.

Umm Dharr's husband is among these men, yet he is different in the sense that the sacred flame of a doubt arises in him when he looks at the Ghifar idol, Manat. He senses that something is not right as he watches his fellow tribesmen worship it with ardency and zeal and ask it for rain to deliver them from the famine that is affecting their people. When they are finally asleep, he arises quietly, picks up a stone, moving in his mind between doubt and uncertainty, goes forward and stares into the eyes of the deity of his time. He sees how blank and empty they are. Full of anger and hatred, he hurls the stone at the idol carved by ignorance and tyranny, hits it and then...nothing. Nothing happens except that he senses freedom, liberation from useless customs. And Umm Dharr shares this feeling with him. Throughout a lifetime of struggle, she stands beside him and supports him and he did the same for her.

Exiled at the end of their life by Caliph Uthman to Rabadhah, poverty increases and hunger becomes more brazen for Umm Dharr and her husband during the last months of their lives. Their goats die one by one. They are faced with death in the loneliness of the desert wilderness. Their daughter dies. They bear it patiently seeing it as a test from God. Their son begins to show the same signs—and then he, too, dies from starvation. They bury him with their own hands.

They are alone now, Umm Dharr and her husband. Poverty, hunger, and age rapidly bring deterioration to Abu Dharr's body. One day, sensing that he has come to the end of his strength, he says to Umm Dharr, "Arise. Perhaps in the wilderness we will find something to quiet our hunger a bit." They both search and search and find nothing. When they return to their tent, Abu Dharr's strength fails. His face shows signs of his approaching death.

Umm Dharr understands. She asks anxiously, "What is happening to you, Abu Dharr?"

"Separation is near," he says. "Leave my corpse on the road and ask some wayfarer to help you bury me."

"The pilgrims have gone," she says with great concern. "There are no wayfarers."

"It can't be," he replies. "Get up and climb to the top of the hill. Someone will come for my death," he tells her.

From the top of the hill Umm Dharr sees three riders approaching from a distance. She signals them. They ride towards her.

"May God bless you," she calls out. "A person is dying here. Help me bury him and receive your reward from God."

"Who is he?" they ask.

"Abu Dharr."

"The companion of God's Messenger?"

"Yea, the same."

"May my mother and father be sacrificed for you, oh Abu Dharr," one of them says.

They stand before him. He is still alive. He says to them, "If any of you work for the caliph or are in the army, do not bury me. If my wife and I had had a cloth to use as my shroud there would have been no need to bother you."

Only one of them is not in the caliph's employment. He says, "I have this cloth with me which my mother wove..." Abu Dharr prays for him and says, "Bury me in that."

One can only ask, if Abu Dharr is buried this way, having spent a whole lifetime in the service of God's Cause, who buried Umm Dharr, who also spent her life serving Him? May God bless her and rest her soul in peace.

IDENTIFICATIONS:
* Ghifar tribe
* Rabadhah
CONSIDER AND DISCUSS:
1. Discuss the bedouin way of life before Islam
 began as exemplified by the Ghifar tribe.
2. Discuss what happens when one destroys an idol.

MUS'AB IBN UMAYR:
The Reader

Mus'ab was born into one of the wealthy families of Makkah. His father was Umayr, a Quraysh from the Banu Abd al-Dar tribe, and his mother was Khannas. He grew into a handsome youth who had developed a refined taste in clothes and perfume. Spending his days in the lap of luxury, he heard the call to Islam echoing throughout Makkah. He joined the first group of Muslim converts to Islam who met at the house of Arqam where they prayed together and discussed the ways to spread Islam.

Accepting Islam, Mus'ab found a new purpose in life. Parties and gatherings of the past lost all meaning for him. He committed himself totally to the Messenger and his mission. Arqam's house now became the center of his world. He regularly attended the secret meetings and listened attentively to the life-giving message of the Messenger.

His parents noticed the change and his mother, in particular, was disturbed by it. To the end of her life she refused to accept his change in ideology and persisted in deriding him and ridiculing his new found faith. Later in his life, Mus'ab tried to explain the faith to her, but she was too proud to accept and too angry that her son had discarded the paganism of his ancestors. Mus'ab was to become a teacher of Islam in Yathrib (Madinah-to-be) before the Messenger migrated. The circumstances leading to this were recorded as follows:

In CE 621, twelve men from Yathrib accepted Islam from the Messenger of God. This covenant is known in Islamic history as the First Aqabah, named after the place where they met outside of Makkah. It is recorded by one of the group, "We pledged our allegiance to the Messenger of God on the night of the First Aqabah, that we would associate nothing with God, that we would neither steal nor commit fornication, nor slay our offspring, nor utter slander; and that we would not disobey him in that which is right." He said to us, "If you fulfill this pledge, then Paradise is yours; and if you commit one of these sins, then receive punishment for it in the next world, that shall serve as expiation. And if you conceal it until the Day of the Resurrection, then it is for God to punish or forgive, even as He will."

After this agreement of the First Aqabah, the Messenger sent Mus'ab to Madinah to became the first teacher of Islam. He was charged with reciting the Quran for them and instructing them in the religion. In Madinah, Mus'ab ibn Umayr was called "The Reader."

When he arrived in Madinah a year before the Messenger's migration, he found a great rivalry existed between the two tribes of the Aws and the Khazraj. It was because of this that those who had become Muslim from the two tribes asked him to lead them in prayer. The house of As'ad ibn Zurarah was opened to him as his home in Yathrib. Moving from house to house, he told the people about the conscious-giving light of Islam. A good number of people converted to Islam, performed the ritual prayers together, and learned to recite the Quran.

He also went to the areas on the outskirts of the city. There he went to a garden by a well called Maraq with As'ad ibn Zurarah and sat in the garden with some of the men who had accepted Islam. Sa'd ibn Mu'adh, leader of his clan, told Usayd, a lesser clan leader, "Go to these fellows who have entered our quarters to make fools of our weak comrades and drive them out. Forbid them to enter our quarters. If it were not that I am related to As'ad who accompanies Mus'ab, I would have saved you the trouble."

Usayd took his lance and went to them. When As'ad saw him, he said to Mus'ab, "This is the chief of his tribe who is coming to you so be true to God with him."

Mus'ab said, "If he will sit down, I will talk to him."

Instead, Usayd stood over them looking furious and asking what they meant by coming to deceive their weaker comrades. He said, "Leave us if you value your lives."

Mus'ab said, "Won't you sit down and listen. If you like what you hear, you can accept it, and if you don't like it, you can forget it."

He agreed that this seemed fair, stuck his lance in the ground, and sat down. Mus'ab explained Islam to him and read him the Quran. Afterwards those present were to say, "By God, before he spoke we recognized Islam in his face by its peaceful glow." Usayd said to Mus'ab, "What a wonderful and beautiful discourse this is! What does one do if he wants to enter this religion?" They told him that he must wash and purify himself and his garments, then bear witness to the truth and pray. He immediately did so and made two prostrations. Then he said, "If you can convert Sa'd ibn Mu'adh, all of his people will follow suit. I will send him to you at once."

He went to Sa'd—who notices a change in his expression—and said, "I have spoken to the two men and I find no harm in them. I forbade them to go on and they said to me, 'We will do what you like.' I told them that the Banu Haritha had gone out against As'ad to kill him because they knew that he was the son of your aunt so as to make you appear a treacherous protector of your guests."

Sa'd, enraged, got up immediately, alarmed at what he had heard. He took his lance from his hand, saying, "By God, I see that you have been utterly ineffective." He went to them in the garden. When he saw them sitting comfortably he knew that Usayd had intended that he should listen to them. He stood over them, looking furious. As'ad had told Mus'ab when they had seen Sa'd coming, "The leader whom his people follow is coming. If he follows you, no two of them will remain behind."

Mus'ab told Sa'd what he had told Usayd. When the people saw Sa'd returning, they said, "We swear by God Sa'd has returned with a different expression." He called his clan and said to them, "I will not speak to a man or woman among you until you believe in God and His Messenger." As a result, every man and woman in his clan joined Islam.

Mus'ab, then, laid the groundwork for the arrival of the Messenger of God (ص). Just two years later the Muslims marched to Badr with Mus'ab as their standard bearer. In 3 AH the Muslims prepared for the Battle of Uhud and Mus'ab was once again made the standard bearer. Mus'ab held his ground even when the battle turned against the Muslims because of the desertion by Muslim forces of their posts of a strategic pass due to their attempt to take spoils from the enemy. He considered it a religious duty to stand firm as the Messenger had commanded. Left alone in the area where the Prophet had ordered the standard bearer to be, he was suddenly surrounded by enemy forces. They cut off his right hand and then his left. He recited over and over again the verse from the Quran, *"Muhammad is only a Messenger of God. There have been Messengers before him."* He held onto the standard with the stumps of his arms and pressed it against his chest, continuously reciting the verse from the Quran. Finally a spear pierced his chest and he fell a martyr like so many Muslims on that day of Uhud.

When the Battle ended, the Messenger moved among the martyrs. At the side of Mus'ab body, he recited from the Quran, *"Among the believers are men who have been true to their covenant with God"* (33:23). Then, addressing the memory of Mus'ab, he said, "When I first saw you at Makkah, no one surpassed your handsome looks and good dress but today your hair is tangled and you have only a plain sheet covering your body. Verily the Messenger of God declares that on the Last Day you will be admitted to the presence of God."

Then, turning to those present, the Messenger said, "Have a last look at the martyrs and send blessings on them. I swear by God who controls my life that whosoever sends blessings on them before the end of the world will be blessed in return."

The profound changes that Islam brought in Mus'ab's life had made him a legend in his own time. This handsome man, growing up in luxury, wearing rich, tasteful clothes, lavishing great care on himself to always be well-groomed, was able to give up all these worldly measures in order to gain the better, eternal world of the spirit, and, through this conversion, serve his fellow human being.

One day in Madinah he had called on the Messenger wearing all he owned—a patched cloth—around his waist. Those who had been present and who had known him as a youth in Makkah, hung their heads as they remembered him then and saw him now. Aware of this, the Messenger said, "Praise belongs to God (*al-hamd Allah*). It is time that mankind learned a lesson and changed their ways. Here is a young man who led the most luxurious life in Makkah, but his love for God and his Messenger and his passion for piety have made him turn his back on all luxury and comfort." Mus'ab's commitment to Islam was an inspiring example for those who find their highest fulfillment in loving and dying in service to His Cause.

IDENTIFICATIONS:
*** First Aqabah**
*** Asad ibn Zurara**
CONSIDER AND DISCUSS:
1. Discuss the spiritual changes Islam brought to Mus'ab.
2. Discuss the verse, "*Among the believers are men who have been true to their covenant with God*" (33:23) as it relates to Mus'ab's life.

ABDULLAH IBN UMM MAKTUM:
The One For Whom His Lord Admonishes Him

Abdullah Umm Maktum, who was blind from birth, was one of the early converts to Islam. He was a cousin of Khadijah bint Khuwaylid, the first wife of God's Messenger and first convert to Islam. His father was Qays ibn Zayd and his mother, Atikah bint Abdullah. His mother came to be known as Umm Maktum ('mother of the concealed one') because she gave birth to a blind child.

Abdullah suffered the persecution of the Quraysh idolaters along with other companions of the Messenger of God (ﷺ). He remained staunch and steadfast in his devotion to the Messenger and his message of Islam. The more he suffered at the hands of the unbelievers, the more firm his faith became and his determination to hold onto the rope of God.

Even though Abdullah was blind, this did not stop him from learning the Quran at every opportunity he found. His insistence and persistence was seen by some as irritating to the Messenger as Abdullah was determined to learn and this often meant taking more of the Messenger's time.

One day, the Messenger was trying to convert the Quraysh leaders to Islam, among whom was Utbah ibn Rabiah and his brother, Shaybah, Abu Jahl, Umayyah ibn Khalaf, and Walid ibn Mughirah, the father of Khalid ibn Walid. While the Messenger was talking to them, Abdullah ibn Umm Maktum approached the Messenger and asked him to recite a certain verse from the Quran. The Messenger frowned and turned away from him. As soon as the Messenger was finished speaking to them, his head began to throb. The following verse was revealed to him at this time: *"The Prophet frowned and turned because there came unto him a blind man (interrupting) but what could tell you that perhaps he might grow (in spiritual understanding)? Or that he might receive admonition and the teaching might profit him? As to those who regard themselves as self-sufficient, to him you do attend, though it is no blame on you if he grows not (in spiritual understanding). But as to him who came to you earnestly striving and with fear (in his heart), of him you were unmindful. By no means should it be so. For it is indeed a Message of instruction. Therefore, let whoso will keep it in remembrance. (It is) in Books held (greatly) in honor, exalted (in dignity), kept pure and holy, (written) by the hands of scribes—honorable, pious, and just"* (80:1-16).

From then on, the Messenger held Abdullah ibn Umm Maktum in special regard. He always asked him about himself, about his needs, and turned his attention to him whenever Abdullah approached him, often saying, "Welcome to him on whose account my Lord has admonished me."

Some say that Abdullah ibn Umm Maktum migrated to Madinah before the Holy Prophet. He worked alongside Mus'ab ibn Umayr teaching the people to recite the Quran and to practice Islam. After the Messenger's migration and the first major battle that the Muslims had to fight against the Quraysh idolaters, known as the Battle of Badr, a verse was revealed which made a distinction between those that go to battle and those that stay at home.

Abdullah ibn Umm Maktum was greatly affected by this verse as he was unable to go to the battles because of his disability. It was painful for him to be denied the higher status. He said to the Prophet, "Oh Messenger of God, if I could go on the *jihad*, I certainly would." He asked God to reveal a message to the Messenger so that those who have disabilities like his do not fall into the lower category of those who stay at home inactive. A verse came: *"No blame is there on the blind, nor is there blame on the lame, nor on the ill (if he joins not the war), but he obeys God and His Messenger—(God) will admit him to Gardens wherein rivers flow; and he who turns back (God) will punish him with a grievous penalty"* (48:17).

He and Bilal were both "Callers to the Ritual Prayer" and "Declarers of the Establishment of the Ritual Prayer." Sometimes Bilal would call to ritual prayer and he would call out the declaration to establish the ritual prayer and sometimes the reverse. Whenever the Holy Prophet went to war, he gave the leadership of the ritual prayer to ibn Umm Maktum while he was gone because ibn Umm Maktum was blind and was thus prohibited from participating in the battles. It is recorded that this happened more than ten times including when the Messenger conquered Makkah.

Abdullah heard that a group of the Quraysh leaders began to go out at night to listen to the Messenger as he was praying in his house. Each one of them chose a place to sit where he could listen. They passed the night listening to him until as the dawn rose, they dispersed. On the way home they met and reproached one another. One said to the other, "Don't do it again for if one of the light-minded fools were to see you, you would arouse suspicion in his mind." Then they left each other. Again, on the second night, everyone of them returned again to his place and they passed the night listening. Then at dawn the same thing happened again. On the third morning they said to one another, "We will not go to our homes until we take a solemn pledge not to return." This they did and then they dispersed. One went to see another and asked him to tell him his opinion of what he had heard from Muhammad. He replied, "By God, I heard things that I know and know what is meant by them and I heard things that I did not know and the meaning of which I did not understand."

They went together to yet a third person's house and asked him the same question. Then Abdullah heard the reasoning for their unbelief. He answered, "What did I hear? We and the Banu Abd al-Manaf have been rivals in honor. They have fed the poor and so have we; they have assumed others' burdens, and so have we; they have been generous and so have we until we have progressed side by side and we became like two horses of equal speed. Then the Abd al-Manaf said, 'We have a Messenger to whom revelation comes from heaven,' and when shall we attain anything like that? By God, we will never believe in him and treat him as truthful."

News spread of the Quraysh's next attempt to turn the Messenger away from his mission. Abdullah was among those who heard the story which is recorded as follows: The Quraysh went to see Abu Talib who was protecting the Messenger. They told him to tell Muhammad that they would give him whatever he wanted if he just gave up his mission. They told him to tell Muhammad that he was one of the noblest of the tribe and held a worthy position in ancestry. He had come to his people with an important matter, dividing their community thereby and ridiculing their customs, insulting their gods and their religion, and declaring that their forefathers were unbelievers. If he wanted money, they would gather for him of their property so that he may be the richest of all; if he desired honor, they would make him their chief (so that no one could decide anything apart from him; if he wanted sovereignty, they would make him king; and if this psychic force (*jinn*) persisted and he could not get rid of it, they would find a physician for him and exhaust their means in getting him cured. " When the Messenger was told this by his uncle, Abu Talib, he said, "I swear by God if they were to offer me the moon in one hand and the sun in the other, I still would not give up my mission."

Utbah ibn Rabi'a listened attentively to the Messenger. He went to the Quraysh to report what he had heard and he said, "Take my advice and do as I do. Leave this man entirely alone for, by God, the words which I have heard will be blazed abroad. If (other) Arabs kill him, others will have rid you of him. If he gets the better of the Arabs, his sovereignty will be your sovereignty, his power your power, and you will be prosperous through him." They said in response, "He has bewitched you with his tongue," to which he responded, "You have my opinion, you must do what you think fit."

Abdullah ibn Umm Maktum was a man of heart, a man who only accepted the highest stage of piety for himself, a man who refused to allow his disability to make him any less. He arranged for a position for himself on the battlefield as the standard bearer saying, "Put me between two rows and hand me the standard to bear. I will hold it and protect it for you and, as I am blind, I cannot run away." Abdullah died in the Battle of Qadisiyyah in AH 14. He had responded to the call of Caliph Umar. Abdullah appeared on the battlefield in full armor, vowing to preserve the standard at the cost of his life. The battle raged for three days in one of the fiercest battles the Muslims ever had to fight. On the third day, the Muslims were victorious over one of the greatest imperial powers of that time. The standard of monotheism (*tawhid*), the worship of the One God, was planted in the earth where it remains in spirit to this day for among the martyrs of the battle was Abdullah ibn Umm Maktum.

IDENTIFICATIONS:
* Umm Maktum
* Banu Abd al-Manaf

CONSIDER AND DISCUSS:

1. How can we apply the lesson in verses 1-16 of Surah 80 to our own life?

2. Discuss the verse 48:17 and how we can apply this to our life.

SALIM, THE FREED SLAVE:
Fights an Apostate of Islam

Salim was of Persian origin, his ancestors having come from the city of Istakhar. He was sold into slavery as a youth and came to be the property of the Messenger's well-known Companion, Abu Hudhayfah. Salim heard from others in Makkah about the Messenger of God. "Where is he?" he wondered. He saw a crowd, went forward, and saw the man in the center. He listened to his words and thought about his life, a perplexing but undoubtedly wondrous one to have heard the revelation from God. The presence of the man, the gravity with which he presented his subject, his charisma, his behavior so fascinated Salim that he became more of an observer and less of a listener. He wondered how he could describe him to others: full of kindness to others in spite of the difficulties he was facing; full of his goodness in spite of the enmity of others; full of serenity in spite of his clear restlessness; full of servitude while clearly in rebellion;

full of love, inspiration, emotions, and finesse of feelings with a heart full of wisdom, logic, vigilance, seriousness, and intellect; all of this and .... alone.

A man, this miracle of a person, threw such turmoil into Salim that he could no longer listen to the words, or, no, he heard, but he was filled with such wonder, such awe for he was hearing the Words of God for the very first time. Salim was not sure he knew what the man was saying but through his strong instincts he sensed that the man was a very special person. He realized that the Words had come from another world. He did not understand truth. He did not comprehend the meaning of the words. He did not know the man, yet he sensed the blessing of revelation, tasted the taste of truth, and sensed the indescribable warmth of faith. He became a Muslim.

The wife of Abu Hudhayfah, set him free and her husband then immediately adopted him as a son. Hudhayfah niece, Fatimah, married him. Fatimah was the daughter of Abu Hudhayfah's brother, Walid, who died at the Battle of Badr when he opposed the Muslim forces. Her grandfather, Utbah, and two of her brothers, Walid and Shaybah, fell at the Battle of Badr at the hands of the Muslims. Her paternal aunt was Hind, the wife of Abu Sufyan who was to take out revenge for her loss at the Battle of Badr by mutilating the body of one of the greatest heroes of Islam and uncle of the Messenger of God, Hamzah ibn Abu Muttalib. What different views these two women had of the Battle of Badr and its effects upon them.

After the Quranic verse was revealed that an adopted son should take the name of his own father and not of the adopted father, Salim came to be called Salim, the freed slave of Abu Hudhayfah. He memorized the Quran and, in addition, had a sweet and pleasing voice such that no matter where he was when he recited the Quran, crowds of people gathered to listen. It was said that once the Messenger called his wife, A'ishah, and she did not respond right away. When she did come, he asked her where she had been. She said, "Messenger of God! A man is outside reciting the Quran in such a beautiful voice that I could not leave."

The Messenger then stepped outside to see who the man was. It was Salim. The Messenger said, "Praise be to God that I have such a gifted person among my followers." Salim was now reciting the verses he had learned from the beloved Messenger of God (ﺹ).

Salim had heard the Messenger recite, *"In the Name of God, the Merciful, the Compassionate. Perish the hands of Abu Lahab, and perish he! His wealth avails him not, neither what he has earned; he shall roast at a flaming fire and his wife, the carrier of the firewood, upon her neck a rope of palm-fiber"* (111:1-5) Hearing the Quran condemning Abu Lahab had given Salim strength for he saw that cruelty and persecution eventually came back to the person who committed it. A person who rages against the truth, burns in his own rage. His hands perish and he along with them. Women, too, who go astray, fuel men's rage to their own loss, like the wife of Abu Lahab. She is choked by a rope she weaves.

Abu Lahab or 'Father of the Flame', the nickname of the uncle of the Messenger of God (ﺹ), had been a relentless enemy of Islam. Salim had heard about the time when the Messenger called together the Quraysh and his own kin to come and listen to his preaching and his warning against the sins of his people. Abu Lahab had flared up and had cursed the Messenger, saying, "Perdition to you!" Abu Lahab died a week after the Quraysh idol-worshippers returned to Makkah from the Battle of Badr where he and the other Quraysh leaders had suffered a major defeat. He had died consumed with grief and his own fiery passions. His wife had been a woman of equally passionate spite and cruelty against the Messenger. She used to tie bundles of thorns with ropes of twisted palm-leaf fiber and carry them and throw them on dark nights in the path where the Messenger would have to walk in order to cause him bodily injury.

And Salim had heard the Messenger recite, *"For the covenants (of security and safeguard enjoyed) by the Quraysh, their covenants (covering) journeys by winter and summer — so let them serve the Lord of this House who has fed them against hunger and secured them from fear"* (106:1-4). Here God is saying to the Quraysh that if they were fond of Makkah and proud of it, if they profited by its central position and its guaranteed security for their caravans of trade and commerce, they should be grateful and worship the One God and accept His Message and His Messenger. The Quraysh were the noblest tribe of Arabia. They were the custodians of the Kabah, the central shrine of Arabia. This gave them a three-fold advantage. First, they had a commanding influence over other tribes because of this. Second, their central position made trade easier for them and gave them both honor and profit. Third, the area around Makkah was a sacred area free from war and private feuds. All of this they owed to the fact that they were the 'Keepers of the Shrine'. As such, they could make agreements of security with the neighboring countries on all sides: Syria, Persia, Yemen, and Abyssinia, protecting their trade routes throughout the year and yet Salim saw that many of them were still not grateful for these blessings from God.

After the death of the Messenger and the spread of apostasy in the Arabian Peninsula, Salim went with the Muslim forces to fight against Musaylimah. As the time for the battle approached, Salim took hold of the standard which he was to hold. A man next to him said, "I respect you as a scholar, but I am afraid you will not be able to defend the honor of the standard you want to carry."

"If I show even the slightest weakness," Salim responded, "I shall be amongst the worst scholars of the Quran."

Salim then marched forth with the troops into battle. He threw himself on the enemy with tremendous courage. As he was mortally wounded, he cried out, *"Muhammad is no more than a Messenger; many were the Messengers that passed away before him. Why, if he should die or is slain, will you turn about on your heels?"* (3:144).

As he was overwhelmed and while he was falling to the ground, another Muslim soldier rushed to grab the banner. As Salim fell to the ground, he asked him, "How is Abu Hudhayfah?"

The response came, "He has joined the ranks of the martyrs."

"And how is the man who questioned my courage?" Salim weakly asked.

"He, too, has been martyred."

"Then," Salim said, "please bury me beside them."

Salim, the freed slave of Abu Hudhayfah rose from his humble origins to become one of the beloved companions of the Messenger of God. He was recorded to have been a man of unbounded faith in God and love for Him. He was always ready to make the greatest sacrifice in order to gain God's satisfaction.

Salim left no children. He willed one-third to the poor and one-third to Abu Hudhayfah's widow. She refused it saying, "I set Salim free to please God. I want no worldly gain for this act of charity." Caliph Abu Bakr then gave all of Salim's wealth to the poor.

IDENTIFICATIONS:
*** Father of the Flame**
*** Quraysh**
CONSIDER AND DISCUSS:
1. Discuss God's anger and curse on Abu Lahab in
Surah 111.
2. Discuss God's admonition to the Quraysh
in Surah 106.

TUFAYL IBN AMR AL-DAWS:
Poet and Leader of His Clan

Tufayl was from the tribe of Aws from the clan of Daws. He was a knowledgeable and intelligent man, a poet and head of his clan. The most intriguing aspect of his life was how he came to accept Islam. He himself told the story: "I went to Makkah to the House of God for the pilgrimage. The leaders of Makkah came at various times to see me. Each and every one of them that I encountered told me the same thing, namely, 'A man has appeared amongst us in our city who has broken from our society, who has caused chaos within our society, who speaks in magical words as a result of which he has caused father to separate from son, brother from brother, wife from husband and husband from wife. We are afraid for you and your tribe. It could be, if you were to hear him, that he would cause you to break with your faith and customs. The best thing to do is not to listen to anything that this man says.' I heard enough of these kinds of words of caution that they had an effect upon me. I decided that the best thing to do was to put cotton in my ears and to keep as far away from Muhammad (ص) as possible. Whenever I went to the Kabah I always put cotton in my ears so that I would not hear anything that he said.

"Then one day I saw him near the Kabah in prayer. I stood near-by. It was as if God wanted me to hear his words. By just hearing a few sentences of his prayer, the words sounded so sweet to me. I had never heard such a beautiful prayer. I said to myself, 'Look at this man. You think that you are a poet and an intelligent person. You can tell the difference between words that are meaningful and those that are not. Why don't you listen to his words and decide for yourself. If they are correct, accept them. If they are incorrect, forget them.'

"He quickly returned to his home. I followed him and I told him what the leaders of Makkah had said to me, adding, 'In spite of all that they said, I was destined somehow to hear your words. Speak to me. Tell me what your goal and purpose is.'

"He recited The Sincerity (*ikhlas*) Surah from the Quran for me. *'In the Name of God, the Merciful, the Compassionate. Say: 'He is God, One. God, the Everlasting Refuge, who has not begotten, and has not been begotten, and equal to Him is not any one'"* (112:1-4) From this Ibn Tufayl must have realized that God is near us; that He cares for us; and we owe our very existence to Him. He is the One and Only God, the Only One to Whom worship is due; all other things that we can think of are His creatures and in no way comparable to Him. He is Eternal, without beginning or end, Absolute, not limited by time or place or circumstance, the Reality before which all other things or places are mere shadows or reflections. Finally, he must have understood that we must not think of Him as having a son or a father. He is not like any other person or thing that we know or can imagine. His qualities and nature are unique.

Ibn Tufayl continues, "Then he recited the Dawn Surah: *'In the Name of God, the Merciful, the Compassionate. Say: I take refuge with the Lord of the Daybreak from the evil of what He has created, from the evil of darkness when it gathers, from the evil of women who blow on knots, from the evil of an envier when he envies'"* (113:1-5). The breaking of darkness and the coming of light can be seen when the darkness of the night is at its darkest, rays of light pierce through and produce the dawn; when the darkness of ignorance is at its worst, the light of God pierces through the soul and gives it enlightenment; non-existence is darkness and life and activity may be typified by light. The source of all true light is God and if we seek Him, we are free from ignorance, superstition, fear, and every kind of evil. Tufayl senses that our trust in God is the refuge from every kind of fear and superstition, every kind of danger and evil. We need to be on guard against physical dangers seen as darkness, psychical dangers within us seen as magic and magical practices, and psychical dangers from without us resulting in a perversion of our will which seeks to destroy any good that we enjoy.

Ibn Tufayl says, "I had never heard such beautiful and meaningful words nor more just commands. I then accepted Islam and became a Muslim." After he became a Muslim, he said to the Prophet, "I hold respect in my clan and am obeyed by them. Ask God to give a sign to them of my sincerity so that in this way, my clan will accept Islam." The Prophet prayed, "Oh God, give Tufayl a sign."

Ibn Tufayl left to rejoin his clan. When he entered the area of his tribe, his father, who was an elderly man, came forward. Ibn Tufayl said, "Father, do not come near me as I am no longer the same person who left here and you are not the same as I am." His father asked, "My son, what has happened to you?" He said, "I have become a Muslim and I have accepted the faith of Muhammad." His father said, "I, too, accept your faith."

His wife came forward. Ibn Tufayl said, "Do not come near

me because I am no longer the same person who left here." She said, "I, also, accept your faith." She became a Muslim. His wife then asked him, "Are you not afraid that our idol will bring harm to me?" Tufayl said, "No. Rest assured that Shara will cause no harm." All of the people in Ibn Tufayl's family accepted Islam, but among the Daws clan, none had.

Ibn Tufayl said that he once again went to Makkah to see the Messenger of God. "I complained to him about the fact that the Daws had not accepted Islam, saying, 'Oh Messenger of God, usury and adultery have kept them from Islam.' The Messenger prayed, 'Oh God! Guide the people of the Daws clan towards me.' Then he said, 'Return to your clan. Be fair and moderate among the people.' "

He returned to his people and with kindness invited the people to Islam. Up until the time that the Messenger migrated to Madinah and the Battles of Badr, Uhud and Khandaq took place, he was inviting his people to Islam. At the time of the Battle of Khaybar, Tufayl migrated with seventy or eighty of his family and tribal members who had accepted Islam. He went from there to the Battle of Khaybar. The Messenger gave them some of the spoils of the war.

Ibn Tufayl then lived in Madinah in service to the Prophet of God. During the Conquest of Makkah, the Messenger was ordered to destroy all of the idols in the various places of idolatry. Tufayl asked for permission to destroy the idol, Dhi al-Kafayn, the idol of his people, which was the special property of Umayr ibn Hammah. He was given permission and he returned to his clan. While he was destroying the idols, he recited this poem: "Oh idols of the unbelievers, I do not worship you. History shows that we preceded you so now I stuff your stomachs with fire."

He returned to Madinah and stayed there until the Messenger died. Subsequently, during the time of Caliph Abu Bakr, the first righteously-guided caliph, he was assigned to fight against the apostates in the Najd. After his victory there he went to Yamamah where the Muslims were fighting. On the way there he saw in a dream that he would not return. And so it happened. This beloved companion of the Holy Prophet, Ibn Tufayl ibn Amr, fought hard in the battle but eventually died a martyr on the battlefield.

IDENTIFICATIONS:

* Shara

* Dhi al-Kafayn

CONSIDER AND DISCUSS:

1. Discuss Ibn Tufayl's reasoning for why he should listen before judging something to be right or wrong.

2. Discuss Surahs 113 and the lesson that can be learned from its message.

MIQDAD IBN AMR AL-ASWAD:
An Emigrant to Abyssinia

Miqdad ibn Aswad, born in Hadramut, was the son of Amr. As a young man he had wounded his rival from another clan and had to flee from his home. He went to Makkah where he was adopted by Ibn al-Aswad who then gave him his name. Later a verse from the Quran was revealed which prohibited this so Miqdad then took the name of his father, Amr. However, he was most often referred to as Miqdad ibn Aswad.

As one of the early converts to Islam, he faced the persecution and torture of the idol-worshippers along with many others. The Messenger of God sought a solution to the pressure being applied against the new converts, especially those who had no large and powerful clan to back them. Among the possible solutions, he chose migration to Abyssinia. News of the just rule of the Christian king there had reached Makkah.

The Messenger of God (ﷺ) chose migration for the pioneer Muslims who hold their belief in the One God with all sincerity.

They were pious people who practiced the highest virtue in Islam —giving to others what they themselves needed—*ithar*. They were prepared to give up their property and even their lives and to forego social position and their ties of kinship if these were to be things which would prevent them from worshipping the One God.

Miqdad ibn-Aswad was among the first group who migrated to Abyssinia. This was the first time in history that a group of Arabs living in Makkah migrated from their tribe and their land by undertaking a group migration to a foreign country. They crossed a sea and ended up in another continent. There they lived among people who were of a different race and religion and under a new kind of social and political order.

The Quran was to reveal four types of migration and Miqdad participated in one of the four types, that is, migration in the way of faith in order to obtain freedom and honor. Miqdad heard of another example of this type of migration when The Cave Surah was revealed to the Prophet, the circumstances for its revelation being recorded as follows: The Quraysh send Uqbah ibn Abu Mu'ayt to the Jewish rabbis in Madinah. The Quraysh said to them, "Ask the Jewish rabbis about Muhammad. Describe him to them and tell them what he says, for they are the first people of the scriptures and have knowledge which we do not possess about the Prophets."

They carried out their instructions and said to the rabbis, "You are the people of the Torah and we have come to you so that you can tell us how to deal with this tribesman of ours." The rabbis said, "Ask him about three things of which we will instruct you. If he gives you the right answer, then he is an authentic Prophet but if he does not, then the man is a rogue, so form your own opinion about him. Ask him what happened to the young men who disappeared in ancient days for they have a marvelous story. Ask him about the mighty traveler who reached the confines of both East and West. Ask him what the spirit is. If he can give you the answer, then follow him, for he is a Prophet. If he cannot, then he is a forger and treat him as you will."

The two men returned to the Quraysh in Makkah and told them that they had a decisive way of dealing with Muhammad and they told them about the three questions. The Quraysh then asked the Messenger the three questions not expecting that he could answer. After a time, God revealed the following: In regard to the young men, God said, *"Have you considered that the dwellers in the Cave .... were wonders from our Signs?"* i.e. there are still more wonderful signs in the proofs given. Then God said, *"When the young men took refuge in the Cave they said, 'Oh Lord, show us kindness and give us guidance by Your command, so We sealed up their hearing in the Cave for many years. Then We roused them in order to test which of the two parties was best at calculating the term of years they had been there"* (18:9-12).

Miqdad knew that the story of the companions of the Cave is the story of individuals who are alone within their corrupt society because they have a different belief system. If they remain with their society, they will surely have to allow themselves to be used by that corrupt society. As they do not want to corrupt their faith, they flee from their society. This is a kind of migration for salvation just as the Messenger told the early Muslims to migrate to Abyssinia for the salvation of the faith. The goal here is not to stay in the city where they were being oppressed because it would mean actively struggling against the corruption and they did not have the means to do this. This is an example of the exceptional state of consciousness reached by the seven persons in this story. It shows that even a few number of people are responsible as individuals. If they cannot serve the people, they should migrate away from them rather than compromise their faith.

In regard to the second question about the mighty traveler, the story of Dhu 'l-Qarnayn was revealed to the Messenger. *"And they will ask you about Dhu'l-Qarnayn. Say: I will recite to you a remembrance of him. Verily We gave him power in the earth and We gave to him the ways and means to all ends...."* (18:83-84).

The third question concerning the Spirit was also answered through revelation when God said concerning the Spirit, *"They will ask you about the Spirit. Say the Spirit is a matter for my Lord and you have only a little knowledge about it"* (17:85). Even though the Messenger of God (ص) successfully answered all three questions and the Jewish rabbis had said that if he does, he is a real Prophet and that they should then follow him, Miqdad saw that they still did not believe.

One day Miqdad was sitting with Abd al-Rahman ibn Awf, a companion of the Prophet and wealthy man. Abd al-Rahman asked Miqdad, "Why don't you get married?"

Miqdad replied, "Will you allow your daughter to marry me?"

Abd al-Rahman was taken aback. He told Miqdad outright that Miqdad was no match for a daughter of his. Miqdad became very upset when he heard this, saying, "Islam makes no such distinctions between the rich and the poor, the high and the low." He wondered why Abd al-Rahman should take such offense at his question.

Miqdad went to see the Messenger and told him what happened. The Messenger said, "I will find a more suitable match for you." Dhiba, a daughter of the Messenger's uncle, agreed to marry Miqdad so that Miqdad gained more than that which he had been refused by Abd al-Rahman.

The Messenger loved Miqdad for his sincerity and enthusiasm for Islam. Miqdad was said to have been a tall, strong man. He was also considered to have been a good soldier and excellent horseman. He devoted his life, as did many of the companions, to Islam. When the Battle of Badr was to take place, all of the companions assured the Messenger of their support. Miqdad stood up and said, "By the Lord Who has made you His Prophet, we will follow you to any part of the world and we will fight under your banner." The Messenger was said to have loved the spirit within these words and prayed for Miqdad. In later years, Miqdad devoted himself to guide people through the Quran and *sunnah* with which he had been very familiar. Many people were reported to have sought out his guidance which he gave willingly.

IDENTIFICATIONS:
* *ithar*
* The Cave Surah
CONSIDER AND DISCUSS:
1. Discuss how the early Muslims must have felt migrating to a new country.
2. Discuss how migration from one's homeland has influenced and changed your life.

JA'FAR IBN ABI TALIB:
Father of the Poor

The son of the Messenger's uncle, Abu Talib, Ja'far at an early age was sent to grow up in the house of his uncle, Abbas, while Ali, his younger brother by ten years, went to live with the Prophet because of the difficult circumstances into which Abu Talib had fallen.

Ja'far married Asma bint Umays, a sister of Maymunah, who later married the Messenger. Ja'far and his wife were among the first converts to Islam. They suffered the cruel treatment at the hands of the Quraysh as had other early followers of Islam. They then migrated to Abyssinia when the Prophet, with great sorrow, gave his permission because it saddened him to see those who say, "Say: God is One. There is no deity but God," be so tortured and humiliated that they have to migrate from their homeland.

While living in Abyssinia, hoping to have left the Quraysh and their oppressive way behind them, two emissaries arrived on behalf of the Quraysh to try to convince the Negus, the just Christian ruler, to send the Muslims back to Makkah. The king refused to do this without first hearing the believers themselves describe their faith.

Ja'far ibn Abi Talib moved forward and made a moving speech about Islam: "Negus, we had been a people in a state of great ignorance, worshipping stone and wooden idols, eating the flesh of dead animals, committing shameful acts, breaking the ties of kinship, mistreating guests, and, if we were strong, we exploited the weak.

"God then sent us a Messenger from among ourselves who is truthful and trustworthy. He asked us to worship the One God and to give up the faith of our ancestors and their idol-worship. He commanded us to speak the truth, to keep our promises, to be kind to our relatives, to help our neighbors, to abstain from killing, to avoid obscenities and bearing false witness against another, not to misuse the property of orphans nor to mistreat women.

"We Muslims accepted his call to this faith of Islam when our people begin to attack us. They tortured and persecuted us, trying to make us renounce our faith. They so oppressed us that life became intolerable under their rule. Hearing about your just rule, we migrated here."

Negus, enthralled by all of this, asked what Ja'far's Prophet had said about God. Ja'far then recited the story of Mary and Jesus from Surah Maryam. *"And mention in the Book Mary when she withdrew from her people to an eastern place, and she took a veil apart from them; then We sent unto her Our Spirit that presented himself to her a man without fault. She said, 'I take refuge in the All-merciful from you! If you fear God...' He said, 'I am but a messenger come from your Lord, to give you a boy most pure.' She said, 'How shall I have a son whom no mortal has touched, neither have I been unchaste?' He said, 'Even so your Lord has said: "Easy is that for Me; and that We may appoint him a sign unto men and a mercy from Us; it is a thing decreed." '*

"So she conceived him, and withdrew with him to a distant place. And the birth pangs surprised her by the trunk of the palm-tree. She

said, 'Would I had died before this, and become a thing forgotten!' But
the one that was below her called to her, 'Nay, do not sorrow; see, your
Lord has set below you a rivulet. Shake also to you the palm-trunk, and
there shall come tumbling upon her dates fresh and ripe. Eat therefore,
and drink, and be comforted; and if you should see any mortal, say, "I
have vowed to the All-merciful a fast, and today I will not speak to any
man." Then she brought the child to her folk carrying him; and they
said, 'Mary, you have surely committed a monstrous thing! Sister of
Aaron, your father was not a wicked man, nor was your mother a woman unchaste.' Mary pointed to the child then; but they said, 'How shall
we speak to one who is still in the cradle, a little child?'_*

*"He said, 'Lo, I am God's servant; God has given me the Book, and
made me a Prophet. Blessed He has made me, wherever I may be; and He
has enjoined me to pray, and to give the alms, so long as I live, and likewise to cherish my mother; He has not made me arrogant, unprosperous.
Peace be upon me, the day I was born, and the day I die, and the day I
am raised up alive!' That is Jesus, son of Mary, in word of truth, concerning which they are doubting. It is not for God to take a son unto
Him. Glory be to Him! When He declares a thing, He but says to it 'Be,'
and it is. Surely God is my Lord, and your Lord; so serve you Him. This
is a straight path"* (19:16-36)

The Negus was moved to tears hearing these words. He said
to the Muslims, "The message of Jesus and that of your Prophet
have come from the same source." He then told the Quraysh to
leave, returning the gifts to them that they had brought for him.

After ten years in Abyssinia, Ja'far and his family moved to
Madinah, the city where the Messenger had migrated. Ja'far was
soon recognized as a person who was very concerned with the
poor, earning himself the nickname of "Father of the Poor."

Some years after his move to Madinah, Ja'far was made second in command of the forces moving against the Byzantines. After the commander, Zayd ibn Haritha, was martyred, Ja'far assumed command and was martyred. News of the death of the
commanders reached the Messenger at Madinah. He was grief-

stricken. He went to see Asma, Ja'far's widow to tell her of the tragic news. When he saw Ja'far's children, he began to cry. Asma asked, "Oh Messenger of God, why do you cry? Do you have news of Ja'far?"

"Yes," he responded. "He has attained martyrdom."

Asma began to mourn. The Messenger said to her, "Oh Asma, don't say anything you will regret and do not beat your chest." He then prayed to God to protect this family of Ja'far and told them that Ja'far had attained Paradise.

He then left her home and went to the home of his daughter, Fatimah, who was also crying. He said to her, "You can easily cry yourself to death for a person like Ja'far. Prepare food for his family because today they are beside themselves with grief." May God rest his soul in peace.

IDENTIFICATIONS:

* Maymunah

* Mary, mother of Jesus

* Jesus ibn Maryam

CONSIDER AND DISCUSS:

1. What would a Christian like the King of Abyssinia find to be common between Islam and his faith in regard to Mary and Jesus?

2. How would you explain the commonalties between Islam and Christianity based on the Quranic verses in this story?

FATIMAH BINT ASAD:
The Messenger's Second Mother

Fatimah bint Asad bin Hashim, the wife of Abu Talib, accept-ed the call to Islam. A few years later she, like the rest of the Hashim and Abd al-Muttalib tribes, were isolated in Makkah and confined to an area in the valley of her husband. The Quraysh had held a meeting and drawn up a document to boy-cott the Banu Hashim and Banu Muttalib tribes after they saw things moving against them, namely, the Messenger's compan-ions had settled in Abyssinia in peace and safety; Umar had be-come a Muslim; he and Hamzah were now on the side of the Mes-senger; and Islam had begun to spread among the tribes.

The Quraysh agreed in the document not to marry the women of the Banu Hashim or Banu Muttalib tribes nor give their women to them to marry nor buy from them nor sell to them. They hung the document up in the middle of the Kabah to remind them of their obligations. As a result, the two clans joined with Fatimah bint Asad and her husband, Abu Talib, in his valley. The families were imprisoned with the exception of Abu Lahab who joined with the enemy. Men, women, and children were placed indiscriminately in the hot, dry valley. The notice written by Abu Jahl in the name of the Quraysh aristocrats and hung on the Kabah wall said: "No one is to have any contact with the Hashim or Abd al-Muttalib tribes. All relationships with them are cut-off. Do not buy anything from them. Do not sell anything to them. Do not marry any of them."

Fatimah bint Asad and her family faced this economic and social boycott. They were forced to live in a rocky prison so that loneliness, poverty, hunger, and the difficulties of life would make them surrender to either the Quraysh idols or death! They had no choice but to bear the torture — both those who had become Muslim like herself and those who had not as yet accepted the faith.

Even those who had not as yet become Muslim from these families put up a united front towards the enemies in order to preserve their family honor. They had faith in Muhammad (ص) as a good person: He sought no personal gain. He had a sense of faith and committment. He did not present himself as being superior to them even though they had not accepted his faith. He acted justly towards all without demanding justice for himself.

Fatimah also knew in her heart that people like the members of her family who had still not accepted Islam, but were willing to bear the hunger and thirst along with her and those members of her family who had accepted Islam, were worth far more than the idol-worshipping intellectuals who sat around the Kabah filled with fear. The intellectuals spoke about philosophy and charity, but when they were presented with a progressive ideology, they refused to accept because it meant being equal with slaves and the deprived. These intellectuals she had seen and listened to spoke about class equality while choosing to act in a way that would protect the wealth of their fathers in order to continue to live in luxury. They chose to act to protect their social position and to avoid opposing the unjust status quo. These intellectuals Fatimah had observed preferred to remain on the side of Abu Jahl and Abu Lahab. They watched the torture of Bilals, Ammars, and Khabbabs and the martyrdom of Sumayyahs and Yasirs without raising a hand to object.

Living in isolation in the hot, dry valley, Fatimah also sensed a new faith had alighted upon her spirit and that of the other believers. The wonders of being human had become clear to her with the appearance of this new movement in her society which was full of danger. She intuited the basis of the movement — experiment, choice, and obligatory disciplines. She could now speak of herself and her responsibilities towards her fellow human beings clearly and without deceit. The liberation she sensed made her aware of both her strengths and her weaknesses. All these things were hidden within the spirit of the movement and yet, wonder upon wonder, it was these very hidden things which were revealed.

Now, in this frightening compound, there were people who were not Muslims and yet they bore the difficulties with patience, silence, and three years of hunger and loneliness. They lived in the shadows of danger. They also took part in God's great revolution of humanity. In this most sensitive moment of the beginning of the history of Islam, they shared the pain, having understood the position of Muhammad and his companions.

The families of the Hashim and Abd al-Muttalib clans were cut off for three years from their city, their people, their freedom, and even their means of livelihood. They were made to live in this confinement. Was it possible to leave the valley in the middle of the night and, hidden from the eyes of the spies of the Quraysh, get some food for the hungry who were waiting in jail? Could it be that a conscience-stricken family member or friend might, out of kindness, bring them some bread? Hunger sometimes reached the point that they took on the image of 'death,' but as they had prepared themselves for martyrdom, they were patient. Sa'd ibn Λbi Waqqas, who was confined with the others, wrote, "Hunger has brought on such dizziness that if at night I kick at a soft and wet material, without even realizing it, I put it in my mouth and suck it. Two years later I still do not know what it was."

One could see under these conditions what passed for the family of the Messenger even if history had said nothing. All of these families bore the difficulties of hunger, loneliness, and poverty for the sake of the Messenger. They patiently bore the cry of a child from the pain of hunger. They remained calm when a sick person moaned in pain from the lack of medicine and food. When an aged person reached the limits of endurance, they said nothing to the Messenger, so as not to cause him greater anguish.

At the same time, in spite of all of the difficulties, they remained loyal and generous in faith and love. All of this showed the expressions of the spirit, of faith, and of human life which greatly affected the sensitive heart of the Messenger. Know for sure that whenever food arrived in the darkness of the night and it was given into the hands of the Messenger to be spread among the people, the share of his wife and daughter was least of all, in order that they not fear for their lives.

The days passed with difficulty in this compound. At night the black tent of darkness fell upon the residents of this mountainous area separated from the life of the city. Weeks, months, and years passed with hardship. They passed slowly over their tired bodies and spirits, but all continued to step in sympathy with each other and with the Messenger.

Then, a short time after the boycott ended, Abu Talib died. Fatimah bint Asad was without her beloved husband. She now had to face the loneliness of widowhood and the man she raised in her home, the Messenger of God (ص), had lost his main support. Her husband had taken the orphan Muhammad into his home and had made up for the missing kindness of his father, mother, and grandfather, Abd al-Muttalib. She and Abu Talib had looked after the young man, Muhammad, and cared for him. Abu Talib found him work in the service of Khadijah. Finally, it was her husband who acted as the father at the marriage of Khadijah and Muhammad (ﷺ). Abu Talib had used all of his influence, personality, and social credit to protect the Prophet. He even bore the three years in confinement, the difficulties and hunger, and remained loyal to his nephew. Now, she had lost Abu Talib, the clan's only protector against the anger, danger, and hatred of the city.

Fatimah had, previous to the death of her husband, borne the loss of Khadijah, the Prophet's wife, who died a short time before Fatimah's beloved husband. Khadijah had lived through ten years of the Messenger's mission, three years of which had been ones of economic and social sanctions. Fatimah had seen and had had her own sense of patience reinforced by her friendship with Khadijah who had also suffered hunger and thirst.

Fatimah would not live many years after the migration to Madinah. She soon became ill. When she was dying, the Messenger went to visit her and said, "Mother, may God bless you. You were my second mother after my own mother died. Even when you were hungry, you made sure I was full. When you had no clothes to wear, you clothed me. You always gave the best food to me, denying it to yourself. You did all of this with the intention of receiving God's satisfaction."

When she died, the Messenger ordered her to be washed and then she was wrapped in his shirt. Someone said to him, "Oh Messenger of God, you have done something for her that you did for no one else."

The Messenger said, "I was an orphan when I was still a young child. She nurtured and raised me. She and Abu Talib were the kindest people to me among all my relatives."

The Messenger told some of his companions to dig the grave

for this companion. He then finished the digging himself. With the help of Abbas and Abu Bakr, they laid her in her grave. May Allah rest her soul in peace.

IDENTIFICATIONS:
* Valley of Abu Talib
* Quraysh aristocrats
CONSIDER AND DISCUSS:
1. Discuss how it must have been living in confinement in the Valley of Abu Talib. If we had the same economic sanctions placed against us, how would we live?
2. Discuss what Abu Talib represented for the Messenger of God (ص).

ALI IBN ABI TALIB:
One Who Grew Up in the Home of the Messenger

Ali ibn Abi Talib, a person who was destined to become the fourth rightly-guided caliph, is described by Ibn Ishaq, the early Muslim historian, as "the first male to believe in the Messenger of God, to pray with him and to believe in his divine message, when he was a boy of ten." Ali grew up in the Messenger's home living with him and his wife Khadijah just as the Messenger had grown up in Ali's house living with Ali's father, Abu Talib, and his wife, Fatimah bint Asad. Poverty had obligated Abu Talib in the later years of his life to allow his son, Ja'far, to grow up in the home of Abbas and his son, Ali, to grow up in the Messenger's house. Ali was present from the time of the first revelation, the moment the Messenger's mission began. He lived through the difficulties, hardships, and persecutions of the first few years of Islam so that he could play the difficult role he was asked to play so the Messenger could migrate to Madinah unnoticed by the idol worshippers. Later, in Madinah, he actively

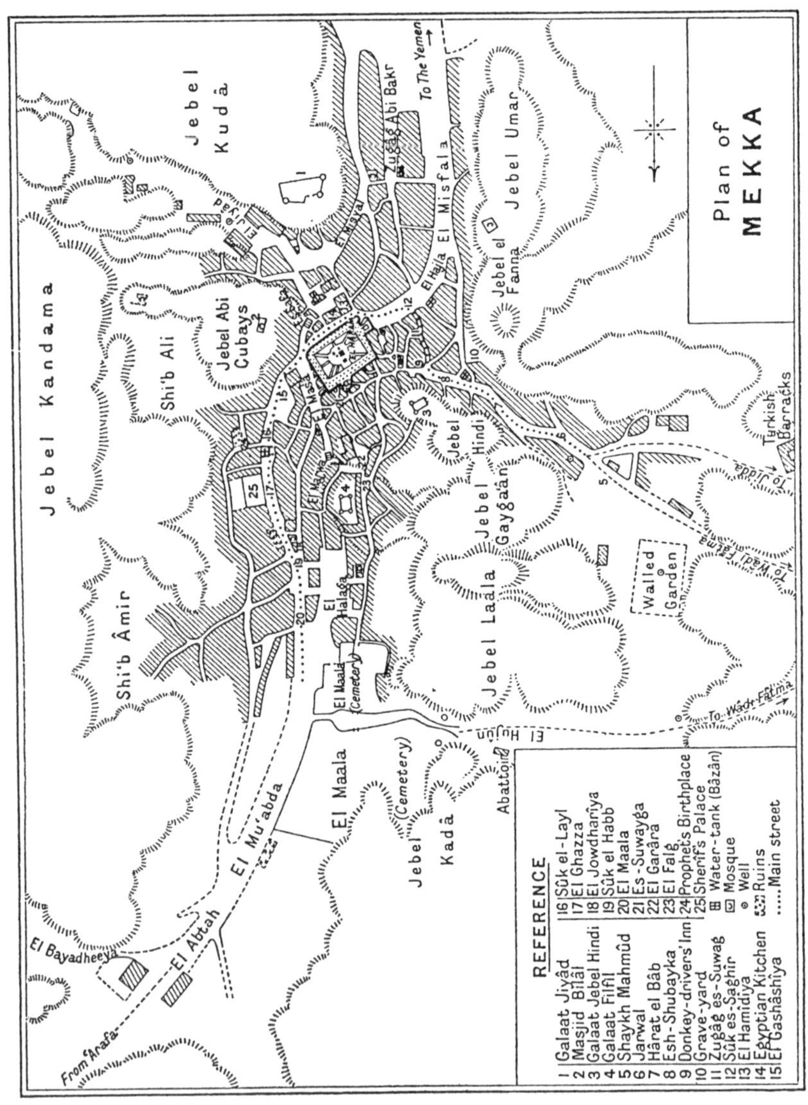

Plan of MEKKA

REFERENCE
1 Galaat Jiyâd
2 Masjid Bilâl
3 Galaat Jebel Hindi
4 Galaat Filfil
5 Shaykh Mahmûd
6 Jarwal
7 Hârat el Bâb
8 Esh-Shubayka
9 Donkey-drivers' Inn
10 Grave-yard
11 Zugâg es-Suwag
12 Sûk es-Saghîr
13 El Hamîdiya
14 Egyptian Kitchen
15 El Gashâshîya
16 Sûk el-Layl
17 El Ghazza
18 El Jowdharîya
19 Sûk el Habb
20 El Maala
21 Es-Suwayga
22 El Garâra
23 El Falg
24 Prophet's Birthplace
25 Sherîf's Palace
   Water-tank (Bâzân)
   Mosque
   Well
   Ruins
   .....Main street

Jebel Kandama
Jebel Ali
Shi'b Ali
Shi'b Âmir
Jebel Abi Cubays
Jebel Kudâ
Zugâg Abi Bakr
To The Yemen
El Hajla
El Misfala
Jebel el Fanna
Jebel Umar
Jebel Hindi
Jebel Gaygâan
Jebel Lagla
Jebel Kadâ (Cemetery)
El Maala
El Mu'abda
El Abtah
El Bayadheeya
From 'Arafa
El Maala (Cemetery)
El Halaga
El Hujûn
Abattoir
Turkish Barracks
To Jidda
To Wadi Fatma
Walled Garden

participated in the battles of Badr, Uhud, Khaybar, the Conquest of Makkah, and Hunayn. He married the Messenger's youngest and most beloved daughter, Fatimah.

Let us concentrate on his role just before the Messenger migrated from Makkah. Its importance as a principle in Islam was confirmed when Muslims adopted the year of the migration to mark the Islamic calendar. This is food for thought because history has continuously made the birth date of the leader of a movement or religion or a great victory the year to begin a calendar. But in Islam none of these—the year of the birth of the Prophet nor the victories of Islam, like the conquest of Makkah—which could have been considered to be the beginning of Islamic political history—was chosen nor even the appointment of the Prophet to prophethood, but rather, once again, migration. It is officially made the marking of the Islamic calendar during the time of Caliph Umar upon Ali ibn Abu Talib's suggestion as the early historian, Tabari, tells us: "Umar ibn Khattab assembled the people and asked them, 'From what day shall we begin our dating?' Ali said, 'From the day on which the Messenger of God migrated and abandoned the land of multitheism.' Umar followed this advice."

Ali had learned of the importance of the concept of migration from the Messenger of God (ﷺ). Makkah had been the land of the Messenger's ancestors, his clan, and his memories in the struggle with the Quraysh which had continued for thirteen years, bearing economic sanctions, being firm against the barriers. The Messenger either had to stay and die in order to preserve the faith and freedom and to carry out his divine and world mission or to migrate.

The only tree that grows in the desert is the family and tribal tree and no individual can live in the desert unless he be under its shadow. Muhammad (ﷺ), with his migration for his Creator, cuts the tree of blood and flesh of the family and tribe that had nurtured him. Muhammad (ﷺ) must leave Makkah but where to go?

Not every place can be like this. He must go wherever the opportunity for living freely is provided and it must be a place which can serve as a base for the struggle in God's cause and we know how the Messenger has been making Yathrib ready for this.

The Prophet gave the order to migrate but the Quraysh were alert to the situation and they sensed the danger. The Messenger ordered the Muslims to leave secretly and a few at a time. The Quraysh tried to prevent the companions from leaving—they returned some of the Emigrants while others continued to live in Madinah. Some had their families taken hostage so they could not leave. The spouses of others refused to let them leave, but the Muslims had made a decision after the Messenger's command. Their decision was to leave the center of ignorance, multitheism, and oppression behind along with their homes, extended families, wealth, and their memories. They chose freedom.

Makkah did not know of the Messenger's decision in regard to himself. Not only were the multitheists not aware of his decision, but even some of his closest companions and family did not know or even guess what his decision was. Most of them thought that just as he had sent his companions to Abyssinia, he sent his companions, who were suffering from persecution and in danger of their lives, to Yathrib. As to himself, they thought because he was connected to the family of Abd al-Manaf, his life was not in danger so he would remain in Makkah and would continue his struggle against the regime.

Abu Bakr readied himself to leave. He went to the Messenger to get his permission. The Messenger in his usual style in these types of situations spoke short, decisive sentences. He said, "No. Don't hurry. Perhaps God is preparing a fellow traveler to accompany you." That is all. Abu Bakr knew that no further discussion was necessary.

At this point only the Messenger, Abu Bakr, and Ali remained in Makkah. Of his Companions, a group was still in Abyssinia, another in Madinah, some in hiding, and some—who did not have any family protection in Makkah—were prisoners of the Quraysh and were being tortured. Some of the young people who had accepted Islam were confined to their homes under the threats of their fathers and elders.

Presently Makkah was empty of Muslims and this was not a normal situation. The Quraysh began to think about it. News from Yathrib increased their anxiety. They heard that the Muslims in Yathrib had all banded together and embraced one another. The Aws and Khazraj tribes, who were in the midst of a 'cease fire,' served the emigrants arriving from Makkah, but they also seemed to be awaiting some great news. Yathrib was completely in the hands of the Messenger's companions.

Clearly under these circumstances, the Messenger would not remain in Makkah with less than a handful of people. The time of patience while bearing persecution and torture had ended. The verse was revealed, *"To those against whom war is made, permission is given (to fight) because they have been wronged—and verily God is Most Powerful for their aid"* (22:39). It announced the beginning of the uprising and positive or constructive struggle. The Messenger would take himself to Yathrib where he would assume the leadership of the city and he would threaten Makkah from outside.

The Quraysh leaders and some of their confederates gathered in their Senate in Dar al-Nadwah. They were holding a council on what to do with Muhammad (ص). One of them suggested, "Let us put him in chains and throw him in prison." This did not receive sufficient votes because another conspirator said that as long as Muhammad was around he was a danger and a threat to them and his companions would come and take him away.

Another suggested, "Let us exile him from the city until we restore order here and we return to how things had been before. Let us remove this nuisance from in our midst and let him go wherever he wants to go." Everyone objected to this suggestion, saying

"Don't you know what powers of persuasion he has and what a fantastic speaker he is. If you do this, he will leave the Arab tribes and will cause others to rise up against you and he will seize the leadership from you."

Finally, Abu Jahl made a decisive suggestion, "I believe that from each tribe a brave young man should be chosen who is known amongst us for his honor. We will give each one of them a sword to attack Muhammad. All of them will act as one body, killing him so that we will be relieved of him. This way everyone will share in the taking of his blood. The family of Abd al-Manaf will not go to war with all of us. They will have to be satisfied with retribution."

The conspirators surrounded his house and watched the Messenger's activities. As the wall of the house was short, they decided to jump over it and crawl into the house and kill the Messenger while he was asleep. A woman called out from inside the house where they were meeting, saying, "You who see yourself as honorable men would do such a thing like jumping over the wall of a house? This will be an eternal disgrace to all Arabs. People will say that we climb over walls to take the daughters of people and that we do not protect our own." Because of this they decided to wait at the door of the courtyard until the Messenger left by the door. They kept the house under surveillance throughout the night. They would see him coming and going and at night they saw that he went to his bed and slept.

In the minds of the conspirators things were coming to an end. The life of the Messenger depended only on a few more quiet hours during which time nothing could happen. The enemy of the Messenger gave him these few final hours because they were certain that the son of Abdullah, who was presently asleep in his small home, had as friends in the city only a 22 or 23 year old youth by the name of Ali and a man in his late 40s by the name of Abu Bakr. *"Or do they say, 'He is a poet for whom we await Fate's un-*

certainty'? Say: 'Await! I shall be awaiting with you' "(52:30-31).

The young men who had seen with their own eyes that the Messenger had gone to his bed and was quietly sleeping were certain that the whole affair would be over at dawn and that Makkah would return to its security and safety. They thought that their fellow idolaters would recapture its honor, its beloved idols whose bases had been shaken during these thirteen years. The certainty of this brought such pleasure to them that they began to recall the words of Muhammad in mockery and ridicule and then they would laugh and tell other stories about him.

Abu Jahl, with his half-wittedness which was particular to people like him, said, "Muhammad thinks that if you follow his way, you will receive the rewards of the Arab and non-Arab. After you have died you will once again be resurrected and you will be given gardens and if you do not follow his way, after you have died, when you are resurrected, you will be thrown into the fires of hell."

At this moment a man passed by them and asked who they were waiting for. They said, "We are waiting for Muhammad." He said, "God has tricked you. Muhammad has escaped your hands." The conspirators go in to look to see if it is not Muhammad who was asleep. Who else could be asleep on his bed and under his covers. As morning comes, they suddenly see that Ali arose from Muhammad's bed.

While the Muslims were in Quba busy building the mosque with the light of hope for the future emanating from their faces, Ali ibn Abi Talib was crossing the desert. He had spent three days from the fateful morning, when the conspirators found him instead of the Messenger in his bed, giving back loans to people to whom the Messenger owed money. He then quickly left the city and began to walk through the burning desert. He was a youth who was in narrow financial straits. His sword was sheathed around his waist, his head lost in thoughts of the future, and warm with faith. He walked during the night and half the day and rested some place during the heat of the day. He arrived in Quba and stayed in the house of Kulthum ibn Hidm where the Messenger was staying.

The Messenger instituted a covenant of brotherhood between his fellow Emigrants and the Helpers when he went to Madinah from Quba. He said, "Let each of you take a brother in God." He himself took Ali ibn Abi Talib by the hand and said, "This is my brother." So God's Messenger, the leader of the God-fearing, the peerless and unequaled, and Ali became brothers. Hamzah, the lion of God, became the brother of Zayd ibn Haritha, the Messenger's freedman. To him Hamzah gave his last testament on the day of Uhud when battle was imminent in case he should meet his death. Ja'far ibn Abu Talib and Mu'adh ibn Jabal became brothers.

Ali ibn Abi Talib lived almost thirty years after the death of the Messenger of God (ص) and died at the hands of an assassin after less than five years as the fourth and last rightly guided caliph. May God rest his soul in peace.

IDENTIFICATIONS:
* Ja'far ibn Abi Talib
* Islamic calendar
CONSIDER AND DISCUSS:
1. Discuss the reason why the date of the Messenger's migration was chosen to mark the beginning of the Islamic calendar.
2. Discuss the significance of 22:39 for the Messenger.

ABU BAKR IBN ABI QUHAFAH:
The Fellow Traveler
of the Messenger of God

Abu Bakr , the man later elected to become the first righteously guided caliph, the first person outside the Messenger's immediate family to accept Islam, was a few years younger than the Messenger of God. Abu Bakr participated in all battles personally led by the Messenger. He was constantly at his side, ready to help with advice and information. At sensitive and critical moments, Abu Bakr was as steady as a rock and did not lose heart. He and the Messenger had a remarkable degree of harmony between them. After the death of Khadijah, the Messenger married Abu Bakr's daughter, A'ishah bint Abu Bakr.

In order to flee from the grip of a city of the enemy and to migrate there must be both self-sacrifice and possibilities and it was because of this that the Messenger kept both Ali and Abu Bakr with him. Ali was a young man who overlooked death when it came between him and God and the Messenger. Abu Bakr was an older, experienced companion who had wealth and influence in the community. They both showed that they were well chosen by the Messenger for their roles in the migration.

The great migration of the Messenger of God (ص) and his companion, Abu Bakr, to Madinah, both opened the closed doors of Madinah to the outside world and, at the same time, familiarized the Makkan emigrants with a new society and new situation. Abu Bakr learned of the importance of migration from the Messenger who decided on it as a new way to provide suitable conditions and new possibilities in his struggle against the Muslims' oppressive political and social environment. They left their place of origin in order to return to it victorious one day.

The Messenger and Abu Bakr took the route to the south instead of the western road which would have led to Yathrib because they knew that the enemy would immediately begin looking for him there. They hid in a cave on Mount Thawr (below Makkah) so that once the enemy got tired of looking for them and returned to the city, they would begin their journey. Abu Bakr had taken care of everything. His son, Abdullah, was assigned to mix with the Quraysh in the city during the day to find out what decisions they had made and what conspiracies they had planned and to come at night and tell the Messenger and his father.

Amr ibn Fahirah, Abu Bakr's servant, was to follow Abdullah with Abu Bakr's sheep to cover over Abdullah's footprints from the city to the cave and back again. Asma, Abu Bakr's daughter, was to bring them food to eat at night. Abdullah ibn Arqat, who was among the multitheists and so was not suspected of any conspiracy, was to take the two camels Abu Bakr had given him and graze them in the desert until the time they wanted to leave for Yathrib. At that point, he was to bring them to the appointed place and to act as a guide.

Once news of the Messenger's escape from Makkah reached the Quraysh, they offered anyone who found the escapees one hundred camels as a reward. This reward brought a lot more people out of the city who dispersed into the desert looking for them than just the enemies of the Messenger. Abu Bakr was anxious. He suddenly heard a group of people near the cave. Shaking with fear, he said, "If these people look below just a little bit, they will see us." The Messenger, calm as always, his head on Abu Bakr's knee, said with a smile and certainty, "What are you saying about these two people whose third one is God?" The Quran says, "*If you do not help (your leader, it is no matter) for God did indeed help him. When the unbelievers drove him out, he had no more than one companion. The two were in the Cave and he said to his companion (Abu Bakr), 'Have no fear for God is with us,' then God sent down His tranquillity upon him (Muhammad) and strengthened him with forces which you saw not and humbled to the depths the word of the unbelievers but the Word of God is exalted to the heights for God is exalted in might, Wise*" (9:40). Faith gave their minds peace and God gave them safety.

By the third day things had quieted down. The search parties had tired of looking. Everyone in the city of Makkah had given up hope of finding them. The way became safe. Abdullah ibn Arqat brought Abu Bakr's two camels. The Messenger was to ride one and Abu Bakr the other and they were to begin the journey with Abu Bakr behind the Messenger. It was a most sensitive and dangerous moment.

But the Messenger was most immediately concerned with something else in spite of the present danger to his life if he were to be found by the searching parties. He turned to Abu Bakr and said, "I will not ride a camel I do not own." Abu Bakr said, "May my mother and father be sacrificed for you, these two belong to you, oh Messenger of God." The Messenger said, "No. How much did you pay for it?" He said such and such an amount. The Messenger said, "I will buy it for that price." Abu Bakr accepted and the Messenger sat upon the camel which he had purchased. They began the journey so that their migration would be completed.

Abu Bakr learned from the Messenger that migration is the breaking of all bonds and ties. An emigrant is in a separate space, a human being unto himself or herself. On one side is the person and his faith and on the other, whatever is other than that, the whole world. Here, Islamic history begins with a caravan of two people and a guide. A great future has fixed its eyes on this Messenger-Emigrant who is presently moving under the heat of the burning sun of the desert. The great superpowers of the world — Iran and Eastern Rome with their life of luxury and extravagance—would look enviously upon this lonely flight which moves during the night along a seemingly pathless road. They travel during the night and a few hours of daylight. When the sun reaches high in the sky and the desert begins to burn beyond what is bearable, they rest behind a stone. Sometimes they will not find even this behind which to rest and they only have the very little shade provided by their two camels in the noonday sun.

They finally arrived in Quba, a town on the outskirts of Madinah where they stayed for a time and build the first mosque. In Madinah itself, the companions of the Messenger, both emigrants and helpers, everyday after the dawn ritual prayer, had gone outside the city and fixed their eyes on the road from Makkah, desirous and anxious. They waited until the time of the noonday sun. The hearts of those who had never seen their Messenger beat for him and were even more anxious.

Once in Madinah, Abu Bakr saw that the Messenger's policy was to stay in touch with the surrounding tribes and to increase his sphere of influence to the furthermost extent possible, allowing whoever wanted to enter Madinah. The Messenger sent out missionaries and ambassadors from Madinah to the outlying areas of the Arabian peninsula, going beyond the borders and establishing contact with Iran, Eastern Rome, Egypt, and Yemen before he was been able to return victorious to Makkah eight years after the migration. Abu Bakr noticed the Messenger's efforts— as a result of his migration—towards opening up all points near and far in the known world to the closed world view of the Arab tribal society which was an extension of migration. Here Abu Bakr saw the effects of intellectual and ideological migration which was confirmed by the Quran:

"Those who believe and who suffer migration and struggle in the path of God — they have the hope of the Mercy of God and God is Oft-forgiving, Most Merciful" (2:218). Abu Bakr realized through this verse that not only is an emigrant placed in the rank of one who struggles in God's Cause (*mujahid*), as the verse shows, but he or she is even given priority. The verse reminded people that after faith, migration is the first and greatest intellectual principle and sacred duty of an individual.

And again, the Quran says: *"...Those who have migrated from their homes and were driven out therefore and suffer harm in My Cause and fought and were slain — verily I will blot out from their iniquities and admit them to Gardens..."* (3:195) In this short verse, Abu Bakr recognized that migration for those who were being oppressed is a factor to consider in seeking a better way of life and an encounter with other situations and this was a truth to which history bears witness.

Abu Bakr heard the verse, *"To those who migrate from their homes in the cause of God, after suffering oppression—We will assuredly give a goodly home in this world: but truly the reward of the Hereafter will be greater if only they realized (this)"* (16:41). Here Abu Bakr realized that the message is to all human beings not to bear emotional ties, social customs, or short sighted political views which may oppress them.

And again, *"When angels take the souls of those who die in sin against their souls, they say, 'In what plight were you?' They reply, 'Weak and oppressed were we in the earth.' They say, 'Was not the earth of God spacious enough for you to move yourselves away (from evil)?'*

Such men will find their abode in hell — what an evil refuge! Except those who are (really) weak and oppressed — men, women, and children — who have no means in their power, nor (a guide post) to direct their way. For them there is hope that God will forgive for God does not blot out (sins) and forgives again and again. He who forsakes his home in the Cause of God finds in the earth many a refuge, wide and spacious. Should he die as a refugee from home for God and His Messenger, his reward becomes due and sure with God and God is Oft-forgiving, most merciful" (4:97-100). Here perhaps it occurred to Abu Bakr that God is giving a command to a person whose heart is inflamed with faith and whose shoulders bear the weight of a heavy responsibility by saying, "You have accepted God's Will, leave your home! Flee! Do not say that you cannot because you are born here. Your home, your family, your city, your tribe is wherever freedom is. Your faith is there."

Abu Bakr knew that those who surrender to a situation in of oppression order to preserve their property or life or wealth have oppressed themselves. They would be deprived from whatever they try to preserve and sell of their freedom and faith. The opposite was also true. Those who give up whatever they have upon the Way of God and migrate will gain more than they lost by migrating. History has shown this to be the case many times as is the case with the Emigrants among the Messenger of God's companions like the upright and truthful (*siddiq*) Abu Bakr. May God rest his soul in peace.

IDENTIFICATIONS:
* Mount Thawr
* Amr ibn Fahirah
CONSIDER AND DISCUSS:
1. Discuss 9:40 and the importance of God's tranquility.
2. Why was it important to the Messenger to buy the
camel he was to ride to Madinah?

ASMA BINT ABU BAKR:
Female Mujahid

Asma bint Abu Bakr, as her name tells us, is the daughter of Abu Bakr. She is also the half-sister of A'ishah who becomes a wife of the Messenger and one of the 'mothers of the believers.' Asma's husband, Zubayr ibn Awwam, was also one of the companions of the Messenger. Her son, Abdullah ibn Zubayr, became well-known for his honesty and his unfailing devotion to Truth.

Asma was among the early converts to Islam. At the time of the migration of the Messenger of God (ﷺ) and her father, Abu Bakr, she was one of the few of his companions left in Makkah who was told about the plan as she was to play an important role in it. Clearly secrecy was of the utmost importance because they had heard of the Quraysh plan to murder the Messenger by one youth from all of the major clans so that the Abd al-Manaf would be obliged to accept retribution for his death rather than blood.

On the night of the departure of the Messenger and her father from Makkah, Asma was the one who prepared food and water for their journey. She looked everywhere for something to put the food in which she could tie, but she could find nothing until she thought of her waistband or *nitaq*. Abu Bakr suggested that she tear it into two pieces. She did this and the Messenger commended her action. From then on she became known as 'the One with the Two Waistbands'.

Even though Asma was pregnant, she made plans to migrate after the Messenger and Abu Bakr arrived safely in Madinah. She was told about the long and difficulty journey ahead for her which her condition would only make more so, but Asma refused to listen. She sensed that He would protect her and her baby. No sooner had she reached Quba, on the outskirts of Madinah, when she gave birth to a son, Abdullah. The Muslims cried out, *"Allah akbar* (God is Greater) and *la ilaha illa lah* (there is no deity but God) in happiness and thanksgiving because Abdullah was the first child to be born to the emigrants in Madinah.

Asma was well known by the other companions as a virtuous and quick-witted woman. Later her son, Abdullah, also described her as being an extremely generous person. He once said, "I have not seen two women more generous than my aunt A'ishah and my mother Asma. Their generosity, however, is expressed in different ways. My aunt A'ishah would accumulate one thing after another until she had gathered what she felt was sufficient and then distribute it all to those in need. My mother, on the other hand, would not keep anything even for the next day. She would distribute whatever she had whenever she had it."

Asma's quick-wittedness along with her sense of honor was well-known. When Abu Bakr, her father, left Makkah for the migration to Madinah, he took all his wealth amounting to some six thousand dirhams with him. He did not leave anything for his family because they were to migrate as soon as he reached Madinah. When Abu Bakr's still idol-worshipping father, Abu Quhafah, heard of his son's departure, he went to his house and said to Asma, "I understand that my son has not only abandoned you, but he has left you no money as well."

In order to save her father's honor, she said, "No, grandfather, in fact he has left us plenty." She took some pebbles and put them in a small cloth in a recess in the wall where they used to put their money. She took the hand of her grandfather—who was now blind — and said, "See how much he has left us." Asma wanted in this way to calm the fears of her grandfather as well as to do something so that he would not try to give them anything of his own wealth. This was because she disliked receiving any assistance from an idol-worshipper even if it was her own grandfather.

Asma had a similar attitude toward her mother, who did not accept Islam. Asma was continuously cautious in situations where she might be required to compromise her faith. In CE 628/ 6 AH, her mother, Qutaylah, who had been divorced from her father, Abu Bakr, in pre-Islamic times, once went to visit her in Madinah. She brought Asma gifts of raisins, butter, and a special kind of fruit. Asma at first refused to admit her mother into the house or to accept the gifts. She sent someone to A'ishah to ask the Messenger how she should relate to her non-Muslim mother. The Messenger sent the message that she should certainly admit her to her house and accept the gifts. On this occasion, the following revelation came to the Messenger, *"God forbids you not, with regard to those who do not fight you because of your faith nor drive you out of your homes, from dealing kindly and justly with them. God loves those who are just. God only forbids you with regard to those who fight you for your faith and drive you from your homes, and support others in driving you out, from turning to them (for friendship and protection). It is such as turn to them (in these circumstances) that do wrong."* (60:8-9)

For Asma and indeed for many other Muslims, life in Madinah was difficult at first, full of hardship and self-sacrifice. Her husband was quite poor. His only major possession at the beginning was a horse he had bought. Asma herself described those early days, "I used to give fodder and water to the horse and groom it. I would grind the grain and make the dough for bread, but I never learned to bake well so the wives of the helpers would bake for me. They were truly good women. I used to carry the grain on my head from Zubayr's plot which the Messenger had given to him to cultivate. It was about eight kilometers from the town's center. One day I was walking on the road carrying the grain on my head when the Messenger and a group of the companions came along the same road. The Messenger called out to me and stopped his camel offering me a place to ride behind him. I felt very embarrassed to even consider traveling with him and I also remembered Zubayr's jealousy—he was the most jealous of men. The Messenger realized that I was uncomfortable with the idea and rode on."

Later Asma related exactly what had happened to her husband Zubayr. He said to her, "By God, it is far more distressing to me that you should have to carry grain for such a long distance than your accepting a ride with the Messenger."

Asma clearly, then, was a person of great sensitivity and devotion. She and her husband both worked very hard together until their situation of living at the poverty level gradually changed. At times, however, Zubayr treated her harshly. Once she went to her father and complained to him about Zubayr. His reply to her was, "My daughter, have patience for if a woman has a righteous husband and he dies and she does not marry after him, they will be brought together again in Paradise."

Zubayr eventually became one of the richest men among the emigrants, but Asma did not allow herself to become extravagant. Her son, Mundhir, once sent her a beautiful, elegant dress from Iraq made of fine and costly material. Asma by this time was blind. She felt the material and said, "It is awful. Send it back to him." Mundhir was upset. He went to her and said, "Mother, it is not transparent." She said, "It may not be transparent, but it is too tight-fitting and shows the contours of my body." Mundhir then bought her another dress that met with her approval and she accepted it.

Asma's final meeting with her son Abdullah has been recorded in early Muslim history as an unforgettable meeting between
two *mujahids*, a son and his mother. Asma showed history the *jihad* of a woman with her sharpness of intelligence, her resolute-
ness, and the power of her faith even at her very advanced age.

Abdullah was in the running for the caliphate after the death
of Yazid ibn Mu'awiyyah. The Hijaz, Egypt, Iran, Khurasan, and
much of Syria were in favor of him becoming the caliph and even
acknowledged him as such. The Umayyids, however, descendants
of Abu Sufyan, continued to contest his caliphate. They gathered
a large army under the command of Hajjaj ibn Yusuf. The two
sides fought difficult battles during which Abdullah ibn Zubayr
displayed great acts of courage and heroism. Many of his supporters, however, could not withstand the continuous strain of
battle. They gradually began to desert him. Finally Abdullah
sought refuge in the Sacred Mosque at Makkah, a refuge which
was denied him and his forces as the Umayyids continued to fight
in the sacred area. It was then that Abdullah slipped out for a
short time to visit his mother, Asma, now an old, blind woman.
He said, "Peace be upon you mother and the mercy and blessings
of God."

"Unto you be peace, Abdullah," she replied. "What is it that
brings you here at this hour while boulders from Hajjaj's catapults
are raining down on your soldiers in the Haram and shaking the
houses of Makkah?"

"I came to seek your advice," he said.

"To seek my advice?" she asked in astonishment. "About
what?"

"My forces have deserted me out of fear of Hajjaj or having
been tempted by what he has to offer. Even my children and my
family have left me. There is only a small group of men left with
me now and however strong and steadfast they may be, they can
only resist for an hour or two more. Messengers of the Banu
Umayyid are now negotiating with me, offering to give me what-

ever worldly possessions I want should I lay down my arms and swear allegiance to Abd ul-Malik ibn Marwan. What do you think I should do?"

Raising her voice, she replied, "It's your affair, Abdullah. You yourself know best. If however you think that you are right and that you are standing up for the Truth, then persevere and continue to fight just as your companions, who were killed under your banner, did. If, however, you desire the world, you will be a miserable person. You will have destroyed yourself and you will have destroyed all that your men have fought for."

"But I will be killed today. There is no doubt about it."

"That is far better for you than that you should voluntarily surrender yourself to Hajjaj and allow some hollow promises of the Banu Umayyid to tempt you."

"I do not fear death. I am only afraid that they will mutilate me," Abdullah responded

"There is nothing after death that man should be afraid of. Skinning does not cause any pain to the slaughtered sheep," Asma said.

Abdullah's face beamed as he said, "What a blessed mother! Blessed be your noble qualities. I have come to you at this hour to hear what I have heard. God knows that I have not weakened or despaired. He bears witness that I have not stood up for what I have out of love for this world and its attractions, but only out of anger for God's Cause which is being disregarded. His limits have been transgressed. I move towards that which is pleasing to you. If I am killed, do not grieve for me, but rather commend me to God."

"I shall only grieve for you," the aging but determined Asma said, "if you are killed in vain and in an unjust cause."

"Rest assured that your son has neither supported an unjust cause, nor committed any detestable deed, nor done any injustice to a Muslim or a non-Muslim living under the protection of an Islamic state (*dhimmi*) and that there is nothing better in his sight than the pleasure of God, the Mighty, the Great. I do not say this to exonerate myself. God knows that I have only said it to make your heart firm and steadfast," Abdullah responded.

"Praise be to God," Asma said, "who has made you act according to what He likes and according to what I like. Come close to me, my son, that I may smell and feel your body for this might be the last earthly meeting with you."

Abdullah knelt before her. She hugged him and smothered his head, his face, and his neck with kisses. Her hands began to squeeze his body when suddenly she withdrew them and asked, "What is this you are wearing, Abdullah?"

"This is my armor," he said.

"This, my son, is not the dress of one who desires martyrdom. Take it off. That will make your movements lighter and quicker. Wear instead the *sirwal* (a long under garment) so that if you are killed your private parts will not be exposed."

Abdullah took off his armor plate and put on the *sirwal*. As he left for the Haram to join the fighting, he said, "Mother, do not deprive me of your prayers."

Raising her hands to heaven, she prayed, "Oh Lord, have mercy on his staying up for long hours and his loud crying in the darkness of the night while people slept...Oh Lord have mercy on his hunger and his thirst on his journeys from Madinah and Makkah while he fasted...Oh Lord, bless his righteousness to his mother and his father...Oh Lord, I commend him to Your cause and I am pleased with whatever You decree for him. And grant me for his sake the reward of those who are patient and who persevere."

By sunset, Abdullah, the first child born to the emigrants after the migration, was dead. Just over ten days later his mother joined him. She was a hundred years old, but age had not blunted the sharpness of her mind.

IDENTIFICATIONS:

* Qutaylah
* Abu Quhafah

CONSIDER AND DISCUSS:

1. Discuss 60:8-9 and how it shows Muslims how to relate to non-Muslims.

2. Discuss the encounter between Asma and her son, Abdullah.

AMMAR YASIR:
The Master Builder

Ammar Yasir suffered the tortures and persecutions of the early Muslims. Had it not been revealed not to accept what is wrong? *"Your Lord knows best those who stray from His path, and those who are rightly guided. Give no heed to the unbelievers: they wish you were pliant, so that they would be pliant. Nor yield to the wretch of many oaths the mischief-making slanderer, the opponent of good, the wicked transgressor, the bully who is besides this of doubtful birth. Though he has wealth and children, when Our revelations are recited to him, he says: 'They are but fables of the ancients.'"* (68:7-15)

And did God not say to strive in His Way? *"That man can have nothing but what he strives for; that (the fruit of) his striving will soon come in sight; then will he be rewarded with a reward complete"* (53:39-41). And to worship the One God: *"Say: 'Men! If you are in doubt concerning my religion (know that) I worship none of those you serve besides Allah, but I serve God Who will cause you to die for I am com-*

manded to be one of the faithful and (I was bidden); "Set your face up-rightly towards religion and do not be a polytheist" (10:104-105). Ammar followed this way as did his mother, Sumayyah, the first martyr in Islam, and his father, who also died under the torture inflicted by Abu Jahl. They did not accept going against God's Way, but strived in His Cause and worshiped the One God alone.

Ammar migrated to Madinah and he was in Quba when the Messenger of God and Abu Bakr arrived from the migration. The sun stood at midpoint and those on lookout were returning to their homes, having given up hope for that day. Suddenly a Jewish man yelled out, "Your grandfather is coming."

Surely Ammar was among the people who went out on the streets. The Messenger and his companion were standing under the shade of a palm tree. Everyone—man and woman, young and old, Jewish and Muslim—all gathered around him. Some of them who had never seen the Messenger did not know who was who between he and Abu Bakr. When the shade of the palm tree was no longer there, Abu Bakr used his cloak to shade the Messenger and then people knew who the Messenger was. The Messenger, went to the home of Kulthum ibn Hidm who was a bachelor and in whose home the emigrant bachelors were staying. Abu Bakr perhaps went to the home of Khayb ibn Asaf.

Ammar Yasir suggested they build a mosque in Quba. This was the first mosque built in Islam. The Messenger himself laid down the stone for the first *qiblah* and then Abu Bakr placed a stone on top of that and then others added to them. This first mosque was without dome, niche, or minaret, nor were there arches supported by pillars nor cloisters.

After the Messenger went to Madinah, one of the first things that he ordered was that a mosque should be built there, as well. It is recorded that Ammar Yasir also helped. The land chosen for the site belonged to two orphans. The Messenger sent for the orphans and their guardians. The land was offered to him as a free gift, but he insisted upon purchasing it, paying more than its value. He ordered the soil leveled and the trees to be felled and laid the foundation for the mosque. Its walls were made of rough stone and unbaked bricks. Trunks of date-trees were supported by a palm-branch roof not higher than seven cubits which was the elevation of Solomon's temple in Jerusalem. All ornament was strictly forbidden. The helpers and the emigrants carried the building materials in their arms from the cemetery of Baqi near the well of Ayyub. The Messenger stayed with Abu Ayyub until the mosque and his apartments were completed and he joined in the work to encourage the Muslims to work and the emigrants and helpers to labor hard. As they build it, the Messenger chanted:

There's no life but the life of the next world.

Oh God, have mercy on the emigrants and the helpers.

At one point while they were building the mosque, Ammar ibn Yasir came to the site overloaded with bricks, saying, "They are killing me. They load me with burdens they cannot bear themselves." Umm Salamah, the Messenger's wife, recorded, "I saw the Messenger run his hand through his hair—for he was a curly-haired man—and say, 'Alas ibn Sumayyah! It is not they who will kill you but a wicked band of men.'" This prophecy is later fulfilled when Ammar is killed at the Battle of Siffin.

The length of this mosque was fifty-four cubits from north to south and sixty-three in breadth. It was hemmed in by apartments on all sides except the western. Until the seventeenth month of the new year, the congregation faced towards the northern wall. After that time, a new revelation turned them in the direction of Makkah, southwards.

Most certainly Ammar heard the first sermon given by the Messenger : "Oh men, send forward (good works) for yourselves. You know, by God, that one of you may be smitten and will leave his flock without a shepherd. Then his Lord will say to him, 'There will be no intermediary to veil him from Him. Did not My Messenger come to you with a message and did not I give you wealth and show you favor? What have you sent forward for yourself?' Then will he look to the right and left and see nothing;

he will look in front of him and see nothing but hell. He who can shield his face from the fire even with a small piece of a date, let him do so; and he who cannot find that, then, with a good word; for the good deed will be rewarded ten-fold, yea, to twice seven hundred-fold. Peace be upon you and God's mercy and blessing.'"

Soon after that, Ammar surely heard the Messenger's second sermon: "Praise be to God whom I praise and whose aid I implore. We take refuge in God from our own sins and from the evil of our acts. He whom God guides none can lead astray; and whom He leads astray none can guide. I testify that there is no God but He alone. He is without partner. The finest speech is the Book of God. He to whom God has made it seem glorious and made him enter Islam after unbelief, who has chosen it above all other speech of men, does prosper. It is the finest speech and the most penetrating. Love what God loves. Love God with all your heart and weary not of the Word of God and its mention. Harden not your hearts from it. Out of everything that God creates, He chooses and select. The actions He chooses he calls good deeds; the people He chooses He calls 'the chosen'; and the speech He chooses He calls good words. From everything that is brought to man, there is the lawful and the unlawful. Worship God and associate nothing with Him. Fear Him as He ought to be feared. Carry out loyally towards God with what you say with your tongues. Love one another in the Spirit of God. Verily God is angered when His covenant is broken. Peace be upon you."

Ammar watched the Messenger spend the greater part of the day in this mosque with his companions, conversing, instructing, and comforting the poor. The apartments of his wives, his family, and his close friends were near by. Here he performed the ritual prayer after the call to pray from the roof. Here he received ambassadors and envoys and the heavenly messages conveyed by the Archangel Gabriel.

Ammar Yasir was considered to have an excellent knowledge

of the Traditions of the Messenger and in addition, owed his renown to his great piety and to his devotion to Islam. He died in CE 657/AH 37 at the Battle of Siffin, fighting on the side of the fourth righteously-guided caliph at an extremely advanced age.

IDENTIFICATIONS:
* Quba
* Yathrib
* Madinah
CONSIDER AND DISCUSS:
1. Discuss the feelings the early Muslims must have had to build the first mosque in Islam.
2. Discuss the feelings the early Muslims must have had to build the Prophet's mosque in Madinah.

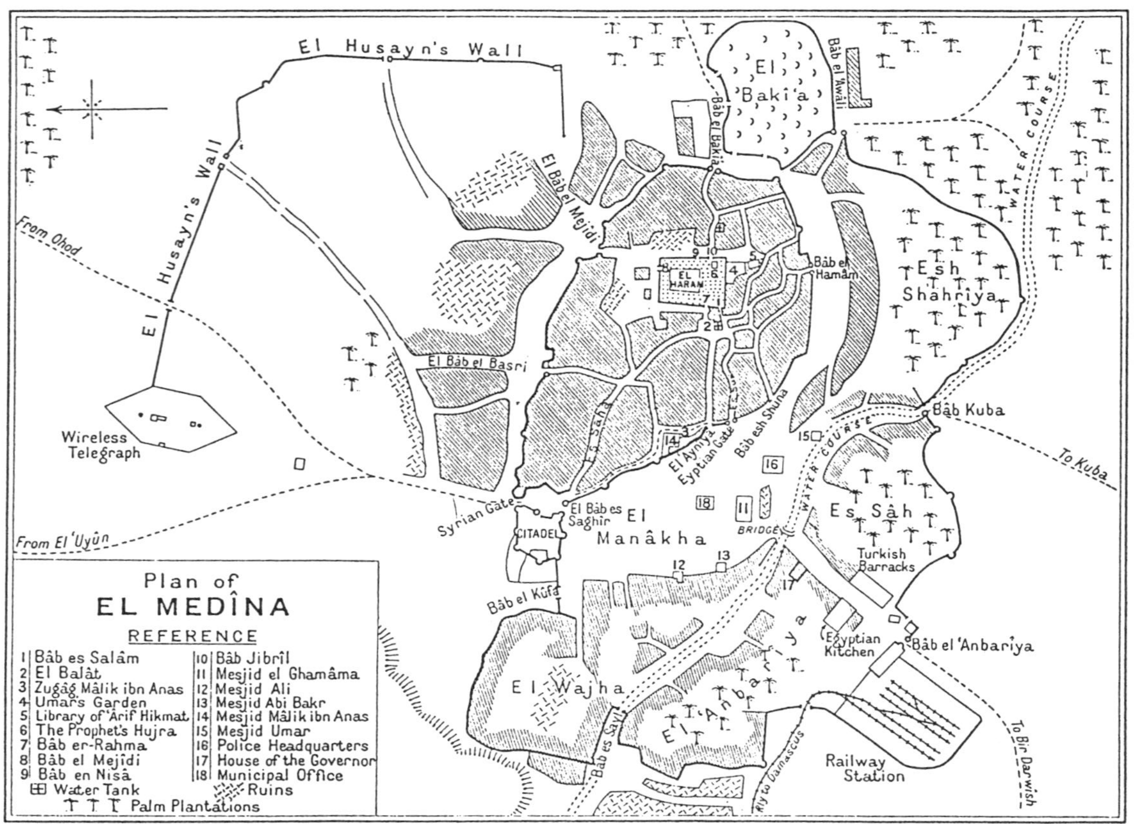

Plan of
EL MEDÎNA
REFERENCE
1 Bâb es Salâm
2 El Balât
3 Zuğâğ Mâlik ibn Anas
4 Umar's Garden
5 Library of 'Arif Hikmat
6 The Prophet's Hujra
7 Bâb er-Rahma
8 Bâb el Mejîdi
9 Bâb en Nisâ
10 Bâb Jibrîl
11 Mesjid el Ghamâma
12 Mesjid Ali
13 Mesjid Abi Bakr
14 Mesjid Mâlik ibn Anas
15 Mesjid Umar
16 Police Headquarters
17 House of the Governor
18 Municipal Office
Water Tank
Ruins
Palm Plantations
El Husayn's Wall
El Bakia
Bâb el 'Awâli
Bâb el Bakia
Bâb el Mejîdi
Bâb el Hamâm
El Haran
Esh Shahriya
WATER COURSE
El Bâb el Basri
El Saha
El 'Aynya
Eyptian Gate
Bâb esh Shuna
Bâb Kuba
To Kuba
Es Sâh
Turkish Barracks
Syrian Gate
CITADEL
El Bâb es El Saghir
Manâkha
BRIDGE
Bâb el Kûfa
Egyptian Kitchen
Bâb el 'Anbariya
El Wajha
Bâb es Sayl
Rly to Damascus
Railway Station
To Bir Darwish
From Ohod
From El 'Uyûn
Wireless Telegraph

ABU DARDA AL-ANSARI AL-KHAZRAJ:
The Ascetic

Abu Darda awoke early one day, as was his habit, and went straight to the part of his house which he had most beautifully decorated because this was where he kept his idol. He greeted it and bowed to it. He rubbed it with his most expensive perfume from his shop in the bazaar and he dressed it in silk. He got ready and left his home at dawn to go to his shop. The streets of Madinah (Yathrib) were crowded that day because the followers of Muhammad were returning from the Battle of Badr. They had brought several prisoners of war from among the Makkans with them. Abu Darda surveyed the crowd and then went up to a youth and asked what happened to his Madinah friend among the Muslims, Abdullah ibn Rawahah.

He was told, "He fought bravely and has returned safely to Madinah."

Abu Darda was very anxious about his close friend, Abdullah

ibn Rawahah. Everyone in Madinah knew of the bond of friendship that had existed for many years between them. Their friendship went back to the time before Islam even came to Yathrib. Ibn Rawahah had accepted Islam, but Abu Darda had not as yet converted but, in spite of this, they were still friends. Abdullah continued to visit Abu Darda and tried to make him see the virtues and blessings of Islam, but to no avail. Abu Darda remained a idol-worshipper, a pagan (*mushrik*). Abdullah was saddened by this and very concerned for his friend.

Abu Darda arrived at his shop and began trading and giving orders to his assistants, unaware of what was happening at his own home. Abdullah ibn Rawahah had gone to visit Abu Darda's home, resolute to take some action. He saw the main gate was open. Umm al-Darda was in the courtyard.

He said to her, "*Salam alaykum* (peace be upon you)."

She responded, "*Wa alaykum salam* (and unto you, peace)."

Abdullah ibn Rawahah asked, "Where is Abu Darda?"

She said that he had gone to his shop and that it would not be long before he returned home.

"Will you allow me to come in?" he asked.

"Please make yourself at home," she said as she continued doing what she had been doing and looking after her children.

Abdullah went to the room where Abu Darda kept his idol. He took out an ax which he had brought with him and began destroying the idol, saying, "Only the One God should be worshiped." When he had smashed the idol to pieces, he left the house. Shortly thereafter, Abu Darda's wife went into the room and saw what has happened. She struck her face in anguish, saying, "Ibn Rawahah, you have brought me ruin."

When Abu Darda returned home, he saw his wife sitting at the door of the room where he kept his idol. She was crying loudly and she looked terrified. "What's wrong with you?" he asked.

"Your brother, Abdullah ibn Rawahah, paid us a visit while you were in your shop and broke your idol, as you see."

Abu Darda looked at the broken idol and was horrified. He was also very angry. He determined to take revenge against his friend. Little by little, however, his anger disappeared and he forgot about seeking revenge. Instead, he began thinking to himself: "If there were any good in this idol, it would have defended itself from injury." He then went straight to Abdullah and together they went to the Prophet, peace be on him. Abu Darda announced his acceptance of the invitation to Islam. He was the last person in his district in Madinah to become a Muslim. From then on, Abu Darda devoted himself completely to Islam.

Having lived many years in Madinah, he had heard of the friendly agreement made by the Messenger between the Muslims and the Jews of Madinah. It was to become known in history as the Constitution of Madinah and the first in the world of its kind.

The agreement between Muslim and non-Muslim said: "In the Name of God, the Merciful, the Compassionate. This is a document from Muhammad the Prophet [governing the relations] between the believers and Muslims of the Quraysh and Yathrib, and those who followed them and joined them and labored with them. They are one community (*ummah*) to the exclusion of all men. The Quraysh emigrants, according to their present custom, shall pay the redemption money within their number and shall redeem their prisoners with the kindness and justice common among believers.

"The Banu Aws, according to their present custom, shall pay the redemption money they paid in the Age of Ignorance... Believers shall not leave anyone destitute among them by not paying his redemption money in kindness. A believer shall not take as an ally the freedman of another Muslim against him. The God-fearing believers shall be against the rebellious or him who seeks to spread injustice or sin or enmity or corruption between believers; the hand of every man shall be against him even if he be a son of one of them. A believer shall not slay a believer for the sake of an unbeliever, nor shall he aid an unbeliever against a believer. God's protection is one. The least of them may give protection to a stranger on their behalf. Believers are friends one to the other to the exclusion of outsiders.

"To the Jew who follows us belongs help and equality. He shall not be wronged nor shall his enemies be aided. The peace of the believers is indivisible. No separate peace shall be made when believers are fighting in the Way of God. Conditions must be fair and equitable to all. In every foray, a rider must take another behind him. The believers must avenge the blood of one another shed in the Way of God. The God-fearing believers enjoy the best and most upright guidance. No multitheist shall take the property or person of Quraysh under his protection nor shall he intervene against a believer. Whosoever is convicted of killing a believer without good reason shall be subject to retaliation unless the next of kin is satisfied with the payment of retribution and the believers shall be against him as one man, and they are bound to take action against him.

"It shall not be lawful to a believer who holds by what is in this document and believes in God and the Last Day to help an evil-doer or to shelter him. The curse of God and His anger on the Day of Resurrection will be upon him if he does, and neither repentance nor ransom will be received from him. Whenever you differ about a matter it must be referred to God and to Muhammad.

"The Jews shall contribute to the cost of war so long as they are fighting alongside the believers. The Jews have their religion and the Muslims have theirs, their freedmen and their persons except those who behave unjustly and sinfully, for they hurt but themselves and their families...The close friends of the Jews are as themselves. None of them shall go out to war save with the permission of Muhammad, but he shall not be prevented from taking revenge for a wound. He who slays a man without warning slays himself and his household unless it be one who has wronged him, for God will accept that.

"The Jews must bear their expenses and the Muslims their expenses. Each must help the other against anyone who attacks the people of this document. They must seek mutual advice and consultation and loyalty as a protection against treachery. A man is not liable for his ally's misdeeds. The wronged must be helped. The Jews must pay with the believers so long as war lasts. Yathrib shall be a sanctuary for the people of this document. A stranger under protection shall be as his host doing no harm and committing no crime. A woman shall only be given protection with the consent of her family. If any dispute or controversy likely to cause trouble should arise it must be referred to God and to Muhammad, the Messenger of God. God accepts what is nearest to piety and goodness in this document. The Quraysh and their helpers shall not be given protection. The contracting parties are bound to help one another against any attack on Yathrib. If they are called to make peace and maintain it, they must do so; and if they make a similar demand on the Muslims, it must be carried out except in the case of a holy war. Every one shall have his portion from the side to which he belongs....

"Loyalty is a protection against treachery. He who acquires anything acquires it for himself. God approves of this document. This deed will not protect the unjust and the sinner. The man who goes forth to fight and the man who stays at home in the city is safe unless he has been unjust and sinned. God is the protector of the good and God-fearing man and Muhammad is the Messenger of God."

Abu Darda's entire being had become filled with belief in the One God and His Messenger and covenants like this first Constitution. He deeply regretted every moment of his life that he had wasted on being an idol-worshipper (polytheist, multitheist, pagan) because he had lost many opportunities to learn and practice Islam. He then realized how much his friends had learned about it in the preceding two or three years in Madinah. They had memorized much of the Quran and devoted themselves to God and

His Messenger. He decided right then and there to spend every effort, day and night, to try to make up for what he had missed. Worship occupied his day and night. His search for knowledge was unceasing. He spent much time memorizing the words of the Quran and trying to understand the profundity of its message. When he saw that business and trade would disturb the sweetness of his worship and keep him from the gatherings of learning, he reduced his involvement without hesitation or regret.

Someone asked him why he did this and he replied, "I had been a merchant before accepting Islam. When I became a Muslim, I wanted to combine both trade and worship, but I was not able to do so. I then decided to move my shop near the mosque so that I could also perform all my daily ritual prayers in the mosque in congregation. I would then still be in trade, but I would do it in a modest way. I want to be among those whom neither trade nor selling distracts from the remembrance of God."

Abu Darda continued to earn his living, but did so in moderation, giving up his luxurious life-style. He only ate what was sufficient to keep him alive. He wore very simple clothes just to cover his body. Once a group of Muslims came to spend the night with him. He gave them hot food which they welcomed. He himself then went to sleep but he had forgotten to give them any blankets. They became anxious, wondering how they would be able to sleep on such a cold night without any blankets. One of them said, "I will go and ask Abu Darda for some blankets." He went to the door of Abu Darda's room and knocked. Abu Darda's wife opened the door to the bedroom. The man could see Abu Darda asleep with only the lightest of clothes on and no blanket covering him.

Abu Darda was reported to have transmitted some Traditions. He was often referred to by early Muslims as a companion of the porch and a number of his sayings of an ascetic character are recorded. He was said to have been the sage (*hakim*) of the early Muslim community. He was best known, however, as an authority on the Quran. He was listed as one of the few who collected revelations during the Messenger's lifetime. After the Messenger's death, he moved to Damascus where he was sent as a judge. There he made it a practice to gather groups in the mosque to whom he taught the Quran, becoming the true founder of the Damascus School. He died in CE 652/AH 32.

IDENTIFICATIONS:

* **Abdullah ibn Rawahah**

* ***mushrik***

* ***hakim***

CONSIDER AND DISCUSS:

1. Study the Constitution of Madinah carefully and discuss it.

2. Discuss Abu Darda's conversion to Islam. How did it change his life style?

FATIMAH BINT MUHAMMAD:
Fatimah, the Radiant

The youngest daughter of the Messenger of God, Fatimah was born some say five years before the Messenger began his mission and some say five years after the mission began. Whichever one it is, it has been recorded that her early years were spent bearing the suffering and difficulties of her father with a very special sympathy. This happened at a time when the birth of daughters was considered to be a disgrace. They were often buried alive to hide the disgrace and where the best son-in-law was considered to be the grave. This view of the female changed with the verse (81:8) and with the way the Messenger of God treated his beloved daughter, the way that he spoke to her, and the way that he praised her.

In Madinah she married Ali ibn Abu Talib after refusing the offer of many others including Abu Bakr and Umar. She and Ali lived next to the Messenger's mosque with just a few meters separating the houses. Whenever the Messenger went on a journey, he knocked at Fatimah's door and said good-bye to her. She was the last person to bid him farewell. Wherever he returned from a journey, she was the first person he sought out. He knocked on her door and asked how she was.

It has been recorded that the Messenger kissed the face and hands of his youngest daughter to teach fathers to love their daughters whom their grandfathers had considered to be a disgrace. He taught them and Muslims who followed them to put aside arrogance and pride and to act with kindness and love towards a woman. He taught a woman to put aside feelings of inferiority, abasement, and deprivation and aim for the highest stage of humanity .

The Messenger spoke about her to others, saying, "The best women in the world were four: Mary (the mother of Jesus), Asiyah (the wife of Pharaoh who nurtured Moses and believed in his message), Khadijah and Fatimah.

Fatimah grew up in poverty, bearing the hardships of her father. Now that she was married, unlike her three sisters who married wealthy men, her house was decorated with love and poverty. Fatimah ground the wheat herself. She baked the bread. She worked in the house. She delivered four children: Hasan, Husayn, Zaynab, and Umm Kulthum. The Messenger was especially close to Hasan and Husayn because they were born in CE 624/AH 2 and CE 625/AH 3 and spend the years of their birth until the ages of nine and eight growing up with their grandfather whereas Zaynab and Umm Kulthum were born in CE 627/AH 5 and CE 628/AH 6 were only six and five when the Messenger of God died.

The Messenger loved his grandchildren very much. One day he entered Fatimah's house as he did everyday when he was in Madinah. He saw that both Ali and Fatimah were asleep and Hasan was hungry and crying. He found nothing to give him. He went to a sheep, milked it, and fed his grandson. One day while passing Fatimah's house, he heard the cries of Husayn. He entered Fatimah's house and he said, shaking, "Don't you understand that his crying causes me pain."

Usamah ibn Zayd related how one day he had business with the Messenger. He knocked at the door and the Messenger answered. As he was talking to him, he realized the Messenger had something hidden under his shirt that he was holding onto with difficulty. When he finished explaining his business, he asked, "What are you holding, Messenger of God?"

The Messenger, his face beaming with delight, pulled apart his shirt and showed that he was holding Hasan and Husayn. Usamah said, "At the same time that he wanted to explain his unusual behavior to me, he could not take his eyes off of them. In a tone full of joy and happiness, he said, as if speaking to himself, 'These are my two sons and the sons of my daughter.' Then in a voice full of amazement and wonder, he continued, 'Oh God, I love these two. Love these two and love those who love them.'"

One day during the ritual prayer, the Messenger went down in prostration. It continued for such a long time that people who were praying behind him began to wonder what had happened. The Messenger had always been swift in ritual prayer. After the ritual prayer had ended, they asked him what had happened. He said, "Husayn had climbed on my back when I had gone down in prostration. As he had the habit of doing this in my home, I could not bring myself to rush him so I waited until he got down. This is why the prostration took so long."

One day the Messenger had been invited some place in the bazaar. While walking with his companions, he saw Husayn with his playmates. The Messenger stood before the children. He extended his hand to his grandson who ran back and forth. The Messenger, laughing and trying to catch him, picked him up. He put one hand on Husayn's back and with the other, held onto his chin and kissed him, saying, "Husayn is from me and I am from Husayn. God loves whoever loves Husayn." His companions looked on in amazement and one said to the other, "The Messenger treats his grandchildren in such a manner. By God, I have a son and I have never kissed him."

The Messenger turned to him and said, "Whoever shows no kindness receives no kindness."

Fatimah entered Makkah at the time of the conquest with her husband and her father. She revisited the city of her birth. She remembered her sisters, Zaynab, Ruqayyah, and Umm Kulthum, all who had died by CE 630/AH 8 and her beloved mother, Khadijah and the Valley of Abu Talib after the confinement of which her mother died.

She returned with the Messenger to Madinah enjoying her father's joy after the victory. He had succeeded in returning to Makkah and His message had spread throughout the peninsula. A few very short years later, however, her joy turned to the most painful sorrow. Her father was bed-ridden.

Looking at him from across the room in his wife A'ishah's house she thought, "He sees in my eyes that I am suffering. His heart bleeds for me, Fatimah, his daughter, his youngest daughter, his only child to outlive him." He indicated to her with his eyes. She went forward and he whispered to her, "I will die."

She picked up her head and described the misery and terror that had overcome her—the terror of his leaving her and the misery of having to live without him was tearing her heart apart." Why is he giving me this message? I am the weakest person here." Then she continued, "His look is fixed on me. His heart bleeds for his youngest daughter who is so close to him. He is indicating again that I should draw near. What could he tell me this time?"

Almost continuing what he had previously told her, he said, "...but you, my daughter, will be the first person from among my family who will join me." Then he added, "Are you satisfied, Fatimah, that you will be the leading woman among all these people?"

She then understood why he told her of his impending death

for after hearing this she found the strength to cry and mourn. He told her to recite the Quran, "Muhammad is no more than a Prophet. Others have been sent before him. If he dies or is killed, you should not go backwards nor return to the reactionary disposition of ancient times."

She recalled the gift which was given to she and Ali at a time of great struggle with poverty and hardship where the frail Fatimah could hardly bear up under the burden of bearing and nurturing her children and taking care of the house. She told Ali of her failing strength. His heart breaking for the life she had been given, he suggested she go to the Messenger and ask him for a female prisoner of war to help manage the things within the house because early on in their marriage they had made a pact that Ali would take care of things outside the house and she would take care of things inside the house.

Fatimah went to see her father. "What is it my daughter?"

"I came to see how you are," was all she could answer. She returned home and told Ali she was too ashamed to ask for something from her father who, himself, had nothing. Ali was stuck with awe at her humility and *ithar*, giving to others what she herself needed. He suggested they return together to the Messenger and Ali would ask for her.

The Messenger answered without hesitation, "No, by God. I cannot give you even a prisoner of war. The stomachs of my companions are hungry and if I find nothing to give them, I have to exchange the prisoners of war for food for them."

Ali and Fatimah thanked him and returned home with empty hands. Both remained silent lost in the thought as to what had made them ask their beloved Messenger for something when he had already given them so much. That night, suddenly the door opened. It was the Messenger of God come to see them. Ali and Fatimah were shivering the darkness and coldness of the night. They had only a thin cloth to cover them which was so short that when they pulled it up to their chins, their feet were exposed and when they covered their feet, their bodies were exposed.

Softly he said to them, "Do not get up from your place." Then he added, "Do you want to know about something which is better than what you have asked of me?"

"Of course, Messenger of God."

"It is something which Gabriel brought for me which I now share with you: after every ritual prayer, say *Allah akbar* (God is Greater), ten times; *al-hamd Allah* (praise belongs to God), ten times and *subhan Allah* (praise be to God), ten times. When you have gone to bed, say *Allah akbar*, thirty-four times and *al-hamd Allah* and *subhan Allah* thirty-three times each."

Fatimah learned something that reached the depths of her being. She was a Muslim who was continuously learning. She was given a Word in place of what she had asked for. This was the wedding present she received from her beloved father, the Messenger of God. Fatimah bint Muhammad joined her father six months after his death. May God rest her soul in peace.

IDENTIFICATIONS:
* Usamah ibn Zayd
* Hasan ibn Ali ibn Abi Talib
* Husayn ibn Ali ibn Abi Talib
* Zaynab bint Ali ibn Abi Talib
* Umm Kulthum bint Ali ibn Abi Talib

CONSIDER AND DISCUSS:
1. Discuss the gift the Messenger gave his daughter and son-in-law.
2. Discuss the Messenger's treatment of his daughter and grandchildren.

ZAYNAB BINT MUHAMMAD:
The Loyal Wife

Zaynab bint Muhammad was the oldest daughter of the Messenger of God. She married Abu 'l-Aas before the mission of the Messenger began. Her sister was married to the son of Abu Lahab also before the mission of the Prophet. After he began to openly preach Islam and speak against the idols of the Quraysh, Abu Lahab's family, not accepting Islam and the teachings of the Messenger and even actively persecuting him, decided that they had actually helped the Prophet by having their son marry his daughter. They decided that they should return his daughter to him so that he would have the responsibility of looking after her himself.

They went to Zaynab's husband, Abu 'l-Aas, and suggested that he do the same thing and divorce the Messenger's daughter. They said that if he divorced Zaynab they would give him any woman he wanted. He refused saying that he did not want any other wife and especially anyone whom they would provide. The son of Abu Lahab was given the same choice. He, however, agreed and divorced the Messenger's daughter, not having consummated the marriage. She then married Uthman ibn Affan who was to become the third righteously-guided caliph.

Even though Abu 'l-Aas was married to the Messenger's daughter, he still had not accepted Islam. Islam had created a division between Zaynab and her husband although they continued to live together in Makkah until the Messenger migrated to Madinah. Abu 'l-Aas joined the Quraysh against the Muslims at Badr. He was captured and remained at Madinah with the Messenger.

When the Makkans sent ransom for their prisoners, Zaynab sent the money for Abu 'l-Aas. With it, she sent a necklace which Khadijah, her mother, had given her on her marriage to Abu 'l-Aas. When the Messenger saw this, he was deeply moved and said to his Companions, "If you would like to let her have her captive husband back and return her money to her, do so." They at once agreed. They released him and sent her money back. However, a condition was imposed on Abu 'l-Aas that he must allow Zaynab to move to Madinah to be with her father. The Messenger sent Zayd ibn Haritha and one of the helpers with instructions to wait in a valley outside of Makkah until Zaynab came and then to accompany her back to him. They left Madinah about a month after the Battle of Badr and waited in the valley.

Once Abu 'l-Aas reached Makkah, he told Zaynab she should go to her father. Once she was ready to leave her husband and Makkah, her brother-in-law took her in a camel-litter in broad daylight and led her out of Makkah. The Quraysh heard of this and overtook them. One of the Quraysh came up to Zaynab and threatened her with his lance. She was pregnant and became very frightened, losing her baby. Her brother-in-law told the Quraysh that if they came near her, he would kill them. The Quraysh fell back. Abu Sufyan then arrived on the scene and told Zaynab's brother-in-law that he did not do the right thing by taking Zaynab out of the city in broad daylight. He said that this had angered the people because of the terrible defeat that they had suffered at the

Battle of Badr. The Quraysh insisted that he and Zaynab should return with them to the city and wait until the feelings of the people died down and then that he should take her secretly out of the city. This is what he did. Finally, one night he took Zaynab secretly out of Makkah and delivered her to Zayd ibn Haritha to take her to Madinah.

Islam, then, further divided Zaynab and her husband. He lived in Makkah and she in Madinah. He left Makkah shortly after she had gone. He went to Syria to trade some of his goods along with goods of the Quraysh he had been given because of his trustworthy nature. Having completed his business in Syria, on his way back to Makkah, one of the Messenger's raiding parties attacked him near Madinah and took all of his goods. He himself managed to escape.

Abu 'l-Aas went to Zaynab's house in Madinah and asked for her protection which she gave without hesitation. He also asked for the goods he was carrying to be given back to him. Zaynab went to the mosque at the time of the morning ritual prayer and cried out from the women's section before her father, the Messenger of God, began the morning prayer, saying, "Know, oh you men, I have given protection to Abu 'l-Aas al-Rabi'."

Once the Messenger finished his prayers, he turned around to face the men and asked them if they had heard what he had heard. When they confirmed that they had, he swore that he knew nothing about the matter until Zaynab so declared, adding, "Every Muslim has the right to give protection on their behalf." He then went to see his daughter and told her to honor her guest but not to allow him to approach her for she was not lawful to him.

The Messenger then sent for the raiding party which had taken the goods of Abu 'l-Aas and said, "This man is related to us as you know and you have taken property of his. If you think well to restore it to him, we should like that; but if you will not, it is booty which God has given you and you have the better right to it." They replied that they were willing to give it all back. They did so, withholding nothing.

Abu 'l-Aas then went to Makkah and paid back the Quraysh merchants what was due to them including those who had given him money. He then asked if anyone of them had any further claim on him. "No," they say, "we have found you both trustworthy and generous." He then said, "I bear witness that there is no deity but God and that Muhammad is his servant and his Messenger. I would have become a Muslim when I was with him, but I feared that you would think that I only wanted to rob you of your property and now that God has restored it to you and I am clear of it, I submit myself to God." He then left for Madinah to join the Muslims.

Zaynab had been separated for many years from her husband. It was recorded that the Messenger restored her marriage according to the first marriage without any new procedure. Zaynab, the loyal wife whose patience and steadfastness in God's Way finally led her husband to accept Islam, died before her father, the Messenger of God (ص). May God rest her soul in peace.

IDENTIFICATIONS:

* Abu l'Aas

* Son of Abu Lahab

CONSIDER AND DISCUSS:

1. Discuss what this story tells you about marriage between a Muslim woman and a non-Muslim man.

2. Discuss Zaynab's loyalty to her husband and her patience.

HAMZAH IBN ABD AL-MUTTALIB:
The Lion of God

Hamzah was known from an early age as a lover of hunting. One day as he was returning from a day of chase, a slave girl, Abu Ammara, greeted him at the gates of Makkah. She told him that Abu Jahl had called Muhammad names and physically abused him. Hamzah was angered hearing this. He knew that he has been too preoccupied with his own pleasures to pay much attention to his nephew and to listen to his message. Hearing what had happened to Muhammad, he began to feel differently. He recalled some of the words Muhammad had told him and some of the verses he had recited for him. He vowed to make up for his previous lack of interest and went directly to the Kabah to find Abu Jahl.

Hamzah walked up to him and struck him. Blood gushed from Abu Jahl's head. His kinsmen rushed forward to protect Abu Jahl crying out, "Hamzah, have you given up the faith of your ancestors?" realizing that Hamzah had suddenly changed and was now actively defending Muhammad against the Quraysh.

Hamzah responded, "I declare my acceptance of Islam. I believe it to be the Truth. I bear witness that Muhammad is the Messenger of God. By God, I will not give up the Truth—try and stop me, if you can." Abu Jahl was shocked to hear Hamzah talk this way, but he called off his friends before they had hurt Hamzah.

Hamzah and Muhammad (ص) were always close. Hamzah's mother was a cousin of Aminah, the Messenger's mother, who had died when the Messenger was but seven years old. Although Hamzah was the Messenger's uncle, they were close in age.

The situation of the Muslims in Makkah improved by Hamzah accepting Islam. He added great weight to their side because of his respect among the Quraysh and his fearless courage. Hamzah was called "Lion of God" by the Muslims because the Quraysh feared him and were not able to persecute the Muslims as they had before Hamzah joined them.

The Messenger clearly recognized Hamzah's military abilities. Hamzah was commanded by the Messenger to lead three raids against the Quraysh caravans after the migration to Madinah. He proved his strength at the Battle of Badr where he and Ali ibn Abu Talib defeated two strongmen from the Quraysh. Seeing the defeat of the warriors, the Quraysh ordered their 3000 strong army to attack the 313 Muslims. One of the Muslims was wearing an ostrich feather in his turban and wielded drawn swords in each hand. This was Hamzah. The Makkans fled from him in panic.

After the defeat of Badr, the Quraysh swore to get even by killing Hamzah in their next battle, but they realized he was too strong a warrior to be able to kill him in regular combat. Abu Sufyan devised a plan. He promised his African slave, Wahshi, his freedom if he killed Hamzah with his javelin while Hamzah was busy in battle.

When the Battle of Uhud began, a well-known Makkan warrior moved forward to challenge a warrior from among the Muslims. Hamzah accepted and easily cut down the Makkan. Full scale battle broke out and Hamzah killed thirty Makkans within seconds of the fighting. The Quraysh then ordered Wahshi to kill Hamzah while Hamzah was busy fighting. Wahshi hid behind a rock, watching Hamzah and holding his poisoned javelin in his hand. Suddenly Hamzah was close by. He threw his deadly javelin and struck down one of the dearest heroes of Islam.

Once the battle was over, Hind, the wife of Abu Sufyan, whose father and brother had been killed by Hamzah in the Battle of Badr, moved towards Hamzah. She mutilated his body, cutting off his ears and nose and then tore open his stomach as she took her revenge against this beloved companion and uncle of the Messenger of God (ص).

Whenever the death of a human being becomes the guarantee for the life of a people, that person's martyrdom is a means for faith to persist. Martyrdom bears witness to the fact that great crimes are being committed against humanity. These crimes include usurpation of political power and ruling people through tyranny. The very fact that martyrdom occurs shows that values of justice, honesty, and truth are being disregarded, forgotten, and brushed aside.

Martyrdom (*shahadat*) is something that those who support the status quo in order to preserve their own interests want to eliminate from people's minds. It symbolizes how things should be and are not. In summary, it is the only form of *jihad*, the only reason for existence when the power of oppressors grows. It is a sign of being present, of being on the social scene. It is a weapon of both attack and defense and the only way by which truth, right, and justice can show resistance to oppression, tyranny, and idolatry.

The human being is created of a mixture of putrid clay and the Spirit of God—a composite formed of the lowest of the low (putrid clay) and the highest of the high (the Spirit of God). The human being, as such a composite, is provided by the Spirit of God with a way of life containing religious precepts. The various kinds of devotions, laws, giving of charity, good deeds, and continuously gaining knowledge about the world as God's creation become spiritual exercises. These spiritual exercises develop a discipline whereby the most base part of the composite human being is strengthened. The inner strength that develops diminishes the satanic elements within in order to allow the divine self within to flourish.

And among these exercises is martyrdom—to be used when all else, all other ways—fails. Martyrdom consists of an action whereby a person like Hamzah suddenly and in a revolutionary move, throws his physical self into the fire of love and faith in order to become light and sacred. It is because of this that a martyr does not need the ritual ablution of death performed and may have no shroud. There will be no accounting on the Day of Judgment by the martyr because any sin has been removed by the martyrdom and the martyr now finds 'presence with his/her Creator'.

As opposed to other cultures where the death of the hero is considered to be an accident imposed upon the hero, a tragedy, here in Islam just fifteen years after the beginning of the revelation to the Messenger of God, death through martyrdom is the highest level that a Muslim can attain. It is a transformation, an elevation of all that it means to be human. It is itself a great responsibility.

In all ages and in all centuries when the believers in an ideology have power, they safeguard their way of life and honor with *jihad*. But when they fall into a weak position, they guarantee their lives, honor, future, and history with martyrdom for in Islam. A martyr is as the heart of history. Just as a heart sends the life-giving blood throughout the body, a martyr, like the heart, sends his life-giving blood to enliven a society that is dying, a society where its young people have turned away, over time, from the faith of their most primary forefathers to follow the errors of their more recent forefathers, a society that is gradually dying, a society that has surrendered itself to the status quo, a society that has forgotten its responsibility to its fellow human being, a society which has forgotten its own human origins, a society that is closed and prevented from movement, change, and transformation. And the greatest miracle that Hamzah's martyrdom and that of so many throughout Islamic history like him, men and women alike, is that it gives a generation of people new faith in itself.

A martyr shows and teaches that he is victorious over the enemy by transmitting the message that he will not stand helpless before oppression nor will he go along with those who say, "I am unable, therefore, I will not participate in battle," nor with those who say, "Victory over anger is realized when anger is overcome." No. A martyr like Hamzah, the Leader of Martyrs, is victorious over the enemy for his name has remained on the lips of all Muslims and his martyrdom, along with that of so many others, has given generation after generation of Muslims throughout history new faith in itself.

Later, after the Battle of Uhud had ended, the Messenger walked through the battlefield looking at each of the martyrs. He saw Hamzah and was horrified at his mutilated body. Overwhelmed with sorrow, he said, "God's blessings be upon you. I well know what a soft spot was in your heart for your relatives. You were a leader among men in acts of kindness." Thus was laid to rest one of the greatest warriors of Islam. May God rest in peace his soul and the soul of all martyrs in God's Way.

IDENTIFICATIONS:
* Battle of Uhud
* Wahshi
CONSIDER AND DISCUSS:
1. Discuss the concept of martyrdom in Islam.
2. Why is a Muslim martyr considered to be the heart of history?

HUMARAH BINT JAHSH IBN R'AB:
The Nurse

Humarah married her cousin Mus'ab Umayr. This couple accepted Islam with all their hearts and never hesitated in taking their faith forward even when it meant self-sacrifice and struggle. They had accepted all of God's commands including those regarding seeking permission to enter the home of another person. They practiced the social customs as expounded in the Quran. In the time before the revelation, the Arab bedouin would enter anyone's house that they wanted, totally unannounced. The bedouin even felt it was an insult to seek permission to enter another's home. Often they did not even put doors on their houses. Humarah and Mus'ab have heard that the Messenger of God said, "In order to announce your entrance to someone's home, call out God's Name in a loud voice" so the practice developed whereby if one wants to enter the home of another, one calls out God's Name to announce one's presence. If no response is obtained after calling out His Name three times, one turns back from entering. Even on being given permission to enter the home of another, a Muslim says, "Ya Allah."

The Quran also regulated the seeking of permission to enter the home of another, saying: (24:27-30)*"Oh you who believe! Enter not houses other than your own, until you have asked permission and greeted those in them; that is best for you in order that you may heed (what is seemly). If you find no one in the house, enter not until permission is given to you. If you are asked to go back, go back. That makes for greater purity for yourselves and God knows well all that you do. It is no fault on your part to enter houses not used for living in which serve some (other) use for you and God has knowledge of what you reveal and what you conceal"* (24:27-30). They practiced it along with the other early Muslims not as a general ruling, but only when they wanted to enter the home of another person.

They were also aware that there were three times of the day that were private to them when everyone had to seek permission to enter their private quarters: before the morning ritual prayer, noon time, and after the late-night ritual prayer. The Quran said: *"O you who believe! Let those whom your right hands possess and the (children) among you who have not come of age ask your permission (before they come to your presence), on three occasions: before morning ritual prayer; the time when you take off your clothes at noon; and after the late-night ritual prayer. These are your three times of undress. Outside those times it is not wrong for you or for them to move about attending to each other. Thus does God make clear the Signs to you for God is full of knowledge and wisdom"* (24:58).

They knew that it was both the believing man and the believing woman who were told to cast down their glance when talking to one another and not to stare in a fixed way at each other. The Quran revealed: *"Say to the believing men that they should lower heir gaze and guard their modesty. That will make for greater purity for them and God is well-acquainted with all that they do"* (24:30). And, again,*"And say to the believing women that they should lover their gaze and guard their modesty; that they should not display their beauty and ornaments except what (must ordinarily) appear thereof; that they should draw their veils over their bosoms and not display their beauty except to their husbands, their fathers, their husbands' fathers, their sons, their husbands' sons, or their sisters' sons or their women, or the slaves whom their right hands possess, or male servants free of physical needs or small children who have no knowledge of sex; and that they should not strike their feet in order to draw attention to their hidden ornaments. And oh you believers! Turn you all together towards God that you may attain bliss"* (24:31).

They knew in their hearts that they were among the children of Adam to whom God spoke when He told them: *"Oh you Children of Adam! We have bestowed clothes upon you to cover your private parts, as well as to be an adornment to you. But the garment of righteousness — that is the best. Such are among the Signs of God that they may receive admonition"* (7:26). They realized that it was not sufficient, according to this verse, to just cover their private parts. Clearly it serves as a necessary beginning because the body is kept pure and beautiful as long as it is not made impure by misuse. In addition to this, however, the verse told them that the best clothing and ornament we have is "clothing" ourselves with piety or righteousness (*taqwa*), God-fearingness which should cover the nakedness of sin and adorn us with virtues.

In order for women to be protected from harm, the Quran said: *"Prophet! Tell your wives and daughters and the believing women that they should cast their outer garments over their persons (when outside). That is most convenient that they should be known (as such) and not molested. And God is Oft-Forgiving, Most Merciful"* (33:59). Humarah knew that the object was not to restrict her liberty, but to protect her from harm and molestation under the conditions then existing in Madinah when this verse was revealed. The verse tells her to cover herself with outer garments when leaving her home, but not that she should be confined to her home like a prisoner.

She and Mus'ab had learned in regard to social etiquette, *"Oh you who believe! When you are told to make room in the assemblies (spread out and) make room. (Ample) room will God provide for you and when you are told to rise up, rise up. God will raise up to (suitable) tasks (and degrees), those of you who believe and who have been granted (true) knowledge. And God knows with all you do"* (58:11). They learned that even when a great and esteemed person joins a group they are not to press forward without discipline nor are other people who have equal rights to be in that group to be shut out. As Muslims they realized that they must spread out for God's earth is spacious and so are His opportunities.

And in response to greetings, (4:86) *"When a (courteous) greeting is offered you, meet it with a greeting even more courteous, or (at least) of equal courtesy. God takes careful account of all things"* (4:86). And, (24:61) *"But if you enter houses, salute each other—a greeting of blessing and purity as from God. Thus does God make clear the Signs to you that you may understand"* (24:61). Humarah and Mus'ab knew that the meaning of the greeting "salam" included the idea of security and permanence which is unknown in this life; soundness, freedom from defects, perfection; preservation, salvation, deliverance; salutation in accord with those around us; resignation in the sense that we are satisfied and not discontented; in addition to the usual meaning of "peace." They learned to always respond to someone who says, "Peace be upon you," with "And upon you be peace."

In regard to pleasing speech, they learned, *"Tell My servants to be courteous in their speech. The devil would sow discord among them; he is the sworn enemy of man"* (17:53). It told them that even to their enemies and the enemies of God they should speak fair because who are they to judge others? Judgment belongs to God alone and amongst themselves they should not entertain suspicions but speak politely according to the best standards of human speech. A false or unkind word may destroy all their efforts at building up a sense of unity between themselves and among others.

They learned that God does not love the arrogant and proud.

"Do not turn away from men with scorn, nor walk proudly on the earth. God does not love the arrogant and the vain-glorious. Rather let your gait be modest and your voice low. The harshest of voices is the braying of the asses" (31:18-19).

And they learned, *"Do not say of anything, 'I will do it tomorrow,' without adding, 'if God wills (insh Allah).' When you forget, remember your Lord and say, 'May God guide me even closer than this to the truth"* (18:23-24).

Humarah and Mus'ab migrated to Madinah. At the time of the Battle of Uhud, Humarah was responsible to provide water and to treat the wounded. The Battle ended. The women came to seek out news of their families but no one would tell them anything, in particular about those killed, until the Messenger of God arrived. He then spoke to them one by one about their families. When it was Humarah's turn, he said, "Humarah, your brother, Abdullah, has been martyred upon the way of God."

Humarah said, "We come from God and to God is the return. May God bless him and forgive him his sins."

Again he said, "Your beloved uncle, Hamzah, has been martyred."

Humarah said the same thing again, "We come from God and to God is the return. May God bless him and forgive him his sins."

The Messenger then said, "Your beloved husband, Mus'ab, has also been martyred.

She said, "What a difficult battle it was."

The Messenger said, "Women have a special place in the hearts of men and they do not see themselves as separate from their wives." He then asked, "Why in regard to Mus'ab did you respond differently than when I told you the news of your brother and your uncle?"

She said in great sorrow, "I remembered his orphaned child."

This brave nurse also helped the wounded in the Battle of Khaybar and the Messenger gave her of the spoils of that battle.

IDENTIFICATIONS:

* Garment of righteousness
* Outer garment

CONSIDER AND DISCUSS:

1. Discuss the social custom revealed in the Quran in regard to seeking permission to enter another's home.

2. Discuss the Quran's command for women to cover themselves when they leave their homes.

SAFIYYAH BINT ABD AL-MUTTALIB:
A Believing Muslim Woman

Safiyyah was an example of a complete woman. She became a Muslim at the beginning of Islam. She gave her allegiance to the Messenger of God and she migrated to Madinah. During the Age of Ignorance she had married Harith ibn Harb, the brother of Abu Sufyan and, then, after his death, she married Awwam ibn Khuwaylid, the brother of Khadijah. She was present at the Battle of Uhud. When the Muslims were defeated, she picked up a spear and hit those that had fled on the forehead, yelling, "Why did you leave the Messenger of God alone?"

The Messenger told her son, Zubayr, to bring her back from the battlefield before she saw the mutilated body of her brother, Hamzah. Zubayr went to her and said, "Mother! The Messenger of God commands you to return."

She asked, "Why? I have heard that they mutilated the body of my brother. This calamity is not important when one is serving

God's Cause. I am satisfied. I will be patient, God-willing."

Zubayr hurried back to the Messenger and told him what she had said. He said, "Leave her alone, then."

Safiyyah reached the body of Hamzah. She looked at his face and she recited the ritual prayer for him. Then she said, "We come from God and to God is the return." The Messenger then ordered that Hamzah's body be buried.

A few years later, the Messenger decided that the Muslims should go to Makkah for the shorter pilgrimage even though they had not been allowed to enter Makkah for six years. The Quraysh were frightened when they saw the 1400 Muslims gathered out-side of Makkah as they were completely unprepared. They agreed that the Muslims could come the next year for the pilgrimage if they left this year without entering Makkah. The Messenger agreed and the Treaty of Hudaybiah was signed.

Not long after its signing, however, the Quraysh idol-wor-shippers broke the Treaty leading to the revelation of The Woman to Be Examined Surah which Safiyyah heard about. A secret letter was sent by an Emigrant from Madinah to the idolaters in Makkah in most friendly terms, seeking their protection on behalf of his children and relatives left behind in Makkah. The letter was intercepted and he confessed the truth. He was forgiven as he told the truth and his motives did not appear to be evil. However a verse was revealed for future guidance to the effect that you can-not be on terms of secret intimacy with the enemies of your faith. If the enemies of your faith are people who seek to destroy your faith and you, do not become intimate with them even to preserve family unity. This is because such intimacy compromises the life and very existence of your community. The verse says, *"Oh you who believe! Take not My enemies and yours as friends (or protectors), offering them (your) love, even though they have rejected the Truth that has come to you and have (on the contrary) driven out the Messenger and yourselves (from your homes), (simply) because you believe in God, your Lord! If you have come out to strive in My Way and to seek My*

Good Pleasure (take them not as friends), holding secret converse of love (and friendship) with them for I know full well all that you conceal and all that you reveal. And any of you that does this has strayed from the Straight Path" (60:1).

Safiyyah learned the example to follow in circumstances like this was that of Abraham. *"There is for you an excellent example (to follow) in Abraham and those with him when they said to their people, 'We are clear of you and of whatever you worship besides God. We have rejected you and there has arisen between us and you, enmity and hatred forever — unless you believe in God and Him alone'"* (60:4). Abraham was tender-hearted and loyal to his father and his people. He warned them against idolatry and sin and prayed for his father and his people but when they became open enemies of God, Abraham entirely dissociated himself from them and left his home, his father, his people, and his country.

According to the Treaty of Hudaybiah, women under guardianship (including married women) who fled from the Quraysh in Makkah to the Prophet's protection in Madinah were to be sent back. Before this verse was revealed, the Quraysh had already broken the treaty and some instruction was necessary as to what the Madinah Muslims should do in those circumstances. Muslim women married to idol-worshipping husbands in Makkah were oppressed for their faith and some of them came to Madinah as refugees. After this verse, they were not to be returned to the custody of the idolatrous husbands at Makkah because the marriage of believing women with non-Muslims was held to be dissolved if the husbands did not accept Islam. In order to appease the husbands who remained idolaters, the dower they had paid their wives who then became Muslim was returned to the husbands. Thus helpless women refugees were to be protected at the cost of the Muslims. Safiyyah heard the verse in this regard which said, *"Oh you who believe! When there come to you believing women refugees, examine (and test) them. God knows best as to their faith. If you ascertain that they are believers, then do not send them back to the unbelievers. They are not lawful wives for the unbelievers nor are the unbelievers lawful husbands for them. But pay the unbelievers what they have spent (on their dower). And there will be no blame on you if you marry them on payment of their dower to them. But hold not to the guardianship of unbelieving women. Ask for what you have spent on their dowers and let the unbelievers ask for what they have spent on the dowers of women who come over to you. Such is the command of God. He judges (with justice) between you. And God is full of knowledge and wisdom"* (60:10).

Then came the verses whereby men and women entering Islam should pledge themselves. The verse relating to women said that they should make a pledge on six points: (1) to worship none but the One True God; (2) not to steal; (3) not to indulge in sex outside the marriage tie; (4) not to commit infanticide (as the idol-worshippers were prone to female infanticide); (5) not to indulge in slander or scandal; and (6) generally to obey the law and principles of Islam. *"Oh Prophet! When believing women come to you to take the oath of allegiance to you, that they will not associate in worship any other thing whatever with God, that they will not steal, that they will not commit adultery, that they will not kill their children, that they will not utter slander, intentionally forging falsehood, and that they will not disobey you in any just matter — then receive their allegiance and pray to God for the forgiveness (of their sins) for God is Oft-Forgiving, Most Merciful"* (60:12).

Safiyyah then well knew that the enemies of her faith who would exterminate she and her faith as they had done with her brother, Hamzah, were not fit objects of her love. She should follow Abraham's example and with those unbelievers who show no rancor, she should deal with them with kindness and justice.

Safiyyah was also present at the Battle of Khaybar. Whenever the Messenger of God went to war, he protected the women and children in the home of Hisam ibn Thabit because the walls around his home were more solid. At the time when there was war between the Jews of the Bani Qurayzah and Muslims because the Bani Qurayzah had broken the treaty, one of the Jews began to loiter around the home of Thabit and watch the women. Safiyyah said to Hisam, "The Muslims are occupied with war and they cannot protect this base. By God, I do not trust this Jew. He may tell the Jews where we are and cause us trouble. The Messenger and his Companions are attending to the battle and are unaware of our situation. Go and kill the Jew."

Hisam said, "I cannot do such a thing."

Safiyyah upon hearing his answer arose, took a weapon, and left the place of refuge. She killed the man and returned to the refuge.

Safiyyah was a very good poetess especially in expressing the sorrow she felt for her loved ones who had been martyred. She died in CE 641/AH 20 at the age of seventy-three. The Caliph Umar said the ritual prayer over her grave. May God rest her soul in peace.

IDENTIFICATIONS:
* Hisam ibn Thabit
* Abraham
CONSIDER AND DISCUSS:
1. Discuss 60:1 and how it relates to a Muslim's life
in the West.
2. Discuss 60:10 and what it implies for a non-Muslim
woman converting to Islam.

SALMAN FARSI:
The Engineer of the Trench

Salman Farsi, the Persian, was one of the early converts to Islam. He told of his early life and how he came to Islam. "I grew up in the town of Isfahan in Persia in the village of Jay. My father was the chief of the village. He was the richest person there and had the largest house. From the time I was born, my father loved me more than he loved any other person. As time went by, his love for me became so strong and overpowering that he feared he would lose me or that something would happen to me so he kept me at home. I became a prisoner in the same way that young girls were kept.

"I became an avid devotee of the Zoroastrian religion so much so that I attained the position of custodian of the fire which we worshiped. My duty was to see that the flames of the fire remained burning and that I did not go out for a single night or day.

"My father had a very large castle which gave an abundant

supply of crops. He himself looked after the estate and the harvest. One day he was busy with his duties and he said to me, 'My son, as you see, I am too busy to go out to the estate now. Go and look after matters there for me today.'

"On my way to the estate I passed a Christian church and the voices at prayer attracted my attention. I had not heard of this religion nor did I know anything about its followers. I walked into the church to see what the people were doing. I was impressed by their manner of praying and I felt drawn to their faith. 'By God, ' I said, 'this is better than ours. I shall not leave them until the sun sets.' I asked and was told that the Christian religion originated in Greater Syria. I did not go to my father's estate that day and night. I returned home. My father met me and asked what I had done. I told him about my meeting with the Christians and how I was impressed by their religion. He was dismayed and said, 'My son, there is nothing good in that religion. Your religion and the religion of your forefathers is better.'

"I insisted, 'No their religion seems to be better.'

"My father became very afraid that I would leave our religion. He kept me locked up and even put a chain on my feet. I managed to send a message to the Christians asking them to inform me of any caravan going to Syria. I unfettered myself and in disguise accompanied the caravan to Syria. There I asked who was the leading person in the Christian religion and was directed to the bishop of the church. I went up to him and said, 'I want to become a Christian and would like to attach myself to your service, learn from you, and pray with you.'

"The bishop agreed and I entered the church in his service. I soon found out, however, that the man was a corrupt person. He would order his followers to give money in charity while holding out the promise of blessing to them. When they gave anything to spend in the Way of God, however, he would hoard it for himself and not give anything to the poor or needy. In this way he amassed a vast quantity of gold. When the bishop died and the

Christians gathered to bury him, I told them of his corrupt practices and, their request, showed them where he kept their donations. When they saw the large jars filled with gold and silver, they said, 'By God, we shall not bury him.' They nailed him on the cross and threw stones at him.

"I continued in the service of the person who replaced him. The new bishop was an ascetic who longed for the Hereafter and engaged in worship day and night. I was very devoted to him and spent many years with him. When he died, I attached myself to various other Christian religious figures. The last one told me about the appearance of a Messenger in the land of the Arabs who would have a reputation for strict honesty and who would accept a gift but would never consume charity for himself.

"A group of Arab leaders from the Kalb tribe passed through the city where I was and I asked them to take me with them to the land of the Arabs in return for whatever money I had. They agreed and I paid them. When we reached near Madinah, they broke their promise and sold me to a Jew. I worked as a servant for him but eventually he sold me to a nephew of his who was from the Banu Qurayzah tribe. This nephew took me with him to Yathrib, the city of palm groves, as it had been described to me. At that time, the Messenger was inviting his people in Makkah to Islam but I heard nothing about him because of the harsh duties which slavery imposed upon me.

"When the Messenger came to Yathrib after the migration, I was at the top of a palm tree belonging to my master, doing some work. My master was sitting under the tree. A nephew of his came up and said, "May God declare war on the Aws and the Khazraj (the two main tribes in Yathrib). By God, they are now gathering at Quba to meet a man who has come today from Makkah and who claims to be a Messenger of God.

"I felt hot flashes as soon as I heard these words and I began to shiver so violently that I was afraid that I might fall on my master. I quickly got down from the tree and spoke to my master's nephew. 'What did you say. Repeat the news for me?'

"My master became very angry with me and struck me, saying, 'What does it matter to you? Go back to what you were doing.'

"That evening I took some dates that I had gathered and went to the place where the Messenger had arrived. I went up to him and said, 'I have heard that you are a righteous man and that you have companions with you who are strangers and are in need. Here is something from me. I see that you are more deserving of it then others.'

"The Messenger ordered his companions to eat but he himself did not eat of it. I gathered some more dates and when the Messenger left Quba for Madinah I went to him and said, 'I noticed that you did not eat of the dates that I brought you. This, however, is a gift for you.' Of this gift of dates, both he and his companions ate."

Salman was released from slavery by the Messenger who paid his Jewish slave-owner a stipulated price and who himself planted an agreed number of date palms to secure his freedom. After accepting Islam, Salman would say when asked who he was the son of, "I am Salman, the son of Islam from the children of Adam."

In 5 AH/ 627 AD, a number of Jews formed a party against the Messenger and they asked the Quraysh to join them. They asked the Jews, "You are the first people of the Book and you know the nature of our dispute with Muhammad (ﷺ). "Is our religion better or his?"

They replied, "Certainly your religion is better than his and you have a better claim to be right."

The Quraysh were pleased with the answer of the Jews and prepared to join them under the leadership of Abu Sufyan. The Messenger was warned of the impending attack. By the time the news had reached him, he had only one week left to prepare the city. He told every one in the oasis what may happen and gave words of encouragement to his followers and told them if they were patient, fear God, and follow His orders, they would be granted victory. Then just as he had done before Uhud, he called his companions for consultation. Many opinions were expressed as to what the best plan of action would be. Finally, Salman stood up and said, 'Oh Messenger of God, in Persia when we fear an attack of horsemen, we surround ourselves with a trench so let us dig a trench about us now." Everyone agreed to the plan with enthusiasm in particular because they did not want a repeat of Uhud.

Time was at a premium and everyone had to work as quickly as possible if no dangerous gaps were to be left in the defenses. The trench did not need to be continuous because at many places there was a long stretch of fortress-like houses at the edge of the city for protection. To the north-west there were masses of rocks which in themselves were impregnable and just needed to be connected to each other. The nearest one, known as Mount Sal', was to be brought within the entrenchments because the ground in front of it was an excellent site for the camp. The trench would bound the camp in the north in a wide sweep from one of the rocky points to the point on the eastern wall of the town. This was to be the longest single stretch of trench and also the most important.

Salman, in addition to initiating the plan, knew exactly how wide and how deep the trench would have to be. As he had worked with the Banu Qurayzah, he knew that they had all the tools he needed and that they were willing to help because of the common enemy. They supplied mattocks, pickaxes, and shovels as well as date-baskets which were strongly woven of palm-fiber and could be used to carry the excavated earth.

The Messenger made each section of the *ummah* responsible for a part of the trench. He worked alongside them. They went home at dawn everyday after the dawn ritual prayer and returned at twilight. He began a chant which reminded them of their building of the mosque in Quba and the mosque in Madinah, saying,

"Oh God, no good is but the good hereafter.

"Forgive the helpers and the emigrants."

And sometimes they chanted:

"Oh God, no life but the life Hereafter

"Have mercy on the helpers and the emigrants."

Everyone reminded each other that time was short. Anyone who slacked off was reprimanded while Salman was admired by everyone because not only was he strong and able-bodied, but he had spent years as a slave digging and carrying earth for the Banu Qurayzah. People would say, "Salman works like ten men," and a friendly rivalry began. The Emigrants said, "Salman is ours," because he had migrated from many homes in search of guidance. The Helpers responded, "He is one of us. We have more right to him." But the Messenger of God said, "Salman is one of us, a member of the people of the House." His suggestion and supervision of the building of the trench helped the Muslims defeat the Quraysh idol-worshippers and their confederates in the Battle of the Trench.

IDENTIFICATIONS:

* Banu Qurayzah

* Aws

* Khazraj

CONSIDER AND DISCUSS:

1. Discuss Salman's conversion to Christianity.

2. Why did Salman then become a Muslim?

UTHMAN IBN AFFAN:
The Generous

Uthman ibn Affan was a member of the Banu Umayyid family who was an early convert to Islam. He was a wealthy merchant and an accomplished man of the world. He married Ruqayyah, the daughter of the Messenger of God and when she died at the time of the Battle of Badr, he married her sister, Umm Kulthum.

After the migration of the Messenger to Madinah, the Muslims were continuously attacked by the Quraysh. Based on the principle that the Kabah was the home of all of the Arab tribes and that the Quraysh did not own it, but rather that they were protectors and guardians of the Kabah and that no Arab could be prevented from making the pilgrimage to the House of Abraham, the Messenger had announced in Dhiqadeh that he intended to make the pilgrimage to the Kabah.

The Messenger endeavored with his words and various movements to show the Arab people that he had no intention of anything military or political. For this very reason, he did not make this journey exclusive to Muslims. A group of the multitheists also accepted his invitation. Each pilgrim was only allowed to bring one sword—which was recommended to have. The minute the Quraysh heard of the Messenger's movement, they went on to the streets—young and old—to pledge to each other never to allow the Messenger to enter Makkah. He arrived outside Makkah with 1400 people. He wanted to send a courier to the Quraysh to tell them that he had no political or military intentions. He called Umar to send him to the Quraysh with the message of why he had come with 1400 people to Hudaybiah. Umar said that he feared for his life with the Quraysh because there was none of his family to protect him there. He pointed out that the Quraysh were well aware of his rough treatment of them. He recommended the Messenger send Uthman ibn Affan. The Messenger sent Uthman to Abu Sufyan and the other chiefs of the Quraysh to tell them that he had come not for war but simply to make pilgrimage to the Kabah.

As Uthman was about to enter Makkah, Aban ibn Sa'id ibn 'Aas met him and gave him his protection until he could deliver the message. Having heard Uthman's delivery of the message from Muhammad (ﷺ), the Quraysh said that Uthman could go round the Kabah if he wanted. He said that he would not go until Muhammad (ﷺ) did so and the Quraysh then held him as a hostage.

There came over the Messenger a state which was comparable to the receiving of revelation but which left him in full control of his faculties. He instructed one of the companions to go through the camp and proclaim, "The Spirit has descended upon the Messenger and commands allegiance, so go forth in the Name of God to make your pledge." As the Messenger was seated under an acacia tree, each one of the companions came forward and gave their allegiance to him. The first one said, "Oh Messenger of God, I pledge my allegiance unto that which is in your soul," and then the others who followed gave the same pledge. The Messenger then said, "I pledge the allegiance of Uthman," who was being held hostage by the idol-worshipping Quraysh. The Messenger put his left hand as the hand of his son-in-law, grasped it with his right hand, and pledged the agreement. Later The Victory (*al-fath*) Surah is revealed in two verses of which God says, *"Verily those whose pledges their allegiance to you do no less than pledge their allegiance to God. The Hand of God is over their hands. Then anyone who violates his oath, does so to the harm of his own soul and anyone who fulfills what he has covenanted with God—God will soon grant him a great reward"* (48:10). *"God was well-pleased with the believers when they pledged allegiance with you beneath the tree. He knew what was in their hearts and sent down the Spirit of Peace unto them, and has given them the promise of a near victory"* (48:18).

The two armies faced each other in an area outside of Makkah known as Hudaybiah. It was a month in which fighting was forbidden and the Messenger took every care not to give any excuse for war to break out so that if war did break out, the Quraysh be blamed for breaking the sanctity of the sacred month otherwise the Messenger would never have agreed to undertake the pilgrimage. He had been victorious from the political and moral point of view and if he were able to enter Makkah, it would circulate among the Arabs to the effect that six years after fleeing Makkah, Muhammad returned with 1400 idol-destroying Muslims to face the Quraysh.

The Quraysh sent Suhayl ibn Umr to conclude a treaty with two other men. The Messenger told Ali to write down the agreement beginning with the words, "In the Name of God, the Merciful, the Compassionate." Suhayl ibn Umr interrupted, saying, "I know not what He is. Write instead *bismik allahuma*, 'In Thy Name, oh God.'" The Messenger agreed. The Messenger continued to dictate to Ali, "These are the terms of the truce between Muhammad, the Messenger of God and Suhayl, the son of Umr..." Again, Suhayl protested. "If we accepted you as the Messenger of

God we would not have prevented you from the House nor would we have fought against you. Write 'Muhammad, the son of Abdullah.'" Ali had already written, "the Messenger of God." Muhammad (ﷺ) told him to strike those words. Ali said he could not do that. The Messenger asked him to point to the words and the Messenger himself struck them out. Then he told Ali to write instead "the son of Abdullah."

The Messenger accepted everything that Suhayl said to the point that the companions all become very angry and yet they were afraid to say anything to the Messenger. The Muslims were disheartened by the fact that they were forbidden from making pilgrimage to the Kabah. They would have to turn back from the gates of Makkah. This was especially difficult for the emigrants. In their view, any kind of peace meant that the Muslims were weak and that the Quraysh were more powerful. They were so disturbed by what was happening that it was as if they were returning from a war defeated and disgraced.

The Treaty was agreed to known as the Treaty of Hudaybiah. It said (1) that there is to be peace between the parties for ten years; (2) that any tribe or person is free to join either party or to make an alliance with it; (3) that if a Quraysh person from Makkah, under the guardianship, joins the Messenger without the guardian's permission, he or she will be sent back to the guardian but the opposite case does not hold; (4) that the Messenger and his group will not enter Makkah this year but that they could enter unarmed the following year.

Then the first unexpected fruit of this agreement appeared. The Quraysh officially accepted Islam and Muslims were free in Makkah to propagate the faith. People, group by group, were to accept Islam there. The Quraysh would allow Muslims to go the next year on pilgrimage to the Kabah. Also, they would allow them to use the caravan and trade routes.

Uthman was released by the Quraysh and the Messenger returned to Madinah. On the way back, The Victory Surah (*al-fath*) was revealed, saying, *"We have given you a clear victory..."* (48:1) and the Messenger was given the promise that the Muslims could enter the Sacred Mosque and perform the rites of the pilgrimage in the next year. No previous victory in Islam had been greater than this victory. The Treaty of Peace abolished war between the Muslims and the Quraysh. People met in safety and consulted with one another. Whoever intellectually understood Islam through reason, embraced Islam. Twice as many people were to enter Islam during the two years while this Treaty was in effect than had previously entered Islam.

Uthman ibn Affan was to become the third rightly guided caliph. He ruled for eleven years and was assassinated in 35 AH/ 656 AD. May God rest his soul in peace.

IDENTIFICATIONS:

* Banu Umayyid

* Ruqayyah

* Hudaybiah

CONSIDER AND DISCUSS:

1. Discuss the concept of allegiance in Islam as revealed in 48:10 and 48:18.

2. Discuss the importance of the Treaty of Hudaybiah.

UMM SALAMAH:
The Wise

She was a woman whose opinions were sought because of her sense of far-sightedness. Umm Salamah's first husband was Abdullah ibn Abd al-Asad. They were among the first to accept Islam. They suffered the persecution of the first Muslims and migrated with the first group to Abyssinia. They later returned to Makkah and when the Messenger migrated to Madinah, Umm Salamah, her husband, and their son prepared to depart from Makkah as well. She told the story herself of what befell them.

"When Abu Salamah (her husband) decided to leave for Madinah, he prepared a camel for me, helped me on it, and placed our son, Salamah, on my lap. My husband then took the lead and went on without stopping or waiting for anything. However, before we had left Makkah some men from my clan stopped us. They said to Abu Salamah, 'You are free to do what you like, but you have no power over your wife. She is our daughter. We will not let her leave.'

"Then they snatched me away from him. My husband's clan, the Banu Abd al-Asad, saw them take me and my child away and they became enraged. 'No, by God' they cried out, 'we will not abandon the boy. He is from among us and we have first claim on him.'

"They took my son and pulled him away from me. Suddenly, in the space of but a few moments, I found myself all alone. My husband had left for Madinah, my son had been taken away by his father's clan, and my own clan, the Banu Makhzum, had overpowered me and had forced me to stay with them.

"I went out every day to the valley where I sat at the place where this tragedy had occurred for a year and I would cry until night came. One day a cousin of mine passed by and saw my state. He went back to my clan and said, 'Why don't you free this poor woman. You have been the cause of her misery sending her husband off and allowing another clan to take her son.'

"Finally their hearts softened and they allowed me to go but then how could I go and leave my son behind? Some realized the position that I was in and they petitioned the Banu Abd al-Asad to allow my son to join me. They finally agreed. I was then afraid to wait for someone to accompany us to Madinah because I feared the same thing may happen all over again. So I started the journey alone with my son. I had just reached Tan'im (three miles from Makkah) when I met Uthman ibn Talhah (a non-Muslim who was keeper of the Kabah for the Quraysh).

"'Where are you going?'

"'I am going to my husband in Madinah,' I answered.

"' Is there anyone with you?'

"'No, except God and my little boy, here.'

"'I will not abandon you until you reach Madinah,' he said.

"He then took the reins of my camel and lead us to just outside Madinah. I never met an Arab more generous and noble than he. Whenever we reached a resting place, he would make my camel kneel down, wait until I had dismounted, led the camel to a tree, and tether it. He would then go and sit in the shade of another tree. After we had rested, he would get the camel ready and again lead us. He did this everyday until we reached Madinah. When we neared Quba (about two miles from Madinah) which belonged to the Banu Amr ibn Awf, he said, 'Your husband is in this village. Enter it with God's blessings.' He then turned back and headed for Makkah." Umm Salamah met her husband and they rejoiced upon seeing each other.

Events began to unfold very quickly for the Muslims. First the Battle of Badr and then Uhud. Abu Salamah participated in both, but at Uhud he was seriously wounded. He told Umm Salamah as she was seeing to his wounds, "I heard the Messenger say one day, 'Surely we are from God and to Him we shall certainly return.'" Then he prayed, "My Lord, give me in return something good from which only You, Exalted and Mighty, can give.'"

Abu Salamah's condition worsened. The Messenger came to see him only to watch him die. He closed the eyes of his companion, raised his hands to the heavens, and prayed, "Oh Lord, grant forgiveness to Abu Salamah. Elevate him among those who are near to You. Take charge of his family at all times. Forgive us and him, oh Lord of the worlds. Widen his grave and make it light for him."

Umm Salamah came to be called Ayyin al-Arab—one who has lost her husband. She had no one in Madinah but her small children. Both the helpers and the emigrants felt a duty towards her. Abu Bakr proposed marriage but she refused. Umar proposed marriage but she refused. The Messenger of God proposed. She said, "I have three characteristics I am a woman who is extremely jealous and I am afraid that you will see in me something that will anger you and cause God to punish me; I am a woman already advanced in age; and I am a woman who has a young family."

The Messenger replied, "Regarding the jealousy you mentioned, I pray to God Almighty for you to be able to let go of it. Regarding the question of your age, I am afflicted with the same problem. Regarding your dependent family, your family is my family."

From that day forward Umm Salamah became one of the 'mothers of the believers' (*umm al-muminun*). After the Treaty of Hudaybiah in March CE 628/AH 6, the companions were very dejected because they felt they had suffered humiliation at the hands of the Quraysh when they were not allowed to make pilgrimage to the Kabah. Once agreement had been reached with the Quraysh, the Messenger told the 1400 or so people with him to offer their sacrifice and cut a piece of their hair or shave their head so as to mark the end of their journey and the beginning of their return.

The people were very reluctant to do so because they felt so disappointed at what had taken place. Umm Salamah saw the Messenger greatly saddened by the fact that the people did not respond to his command. She said, "Don't insist. It is very difficult for them to bear this peace treaty. Just go and do what you know you have to do without saying anything to anyone—sacrifice your animal and shave your head." On the suggestion of Umm Salamah, the Messenger got up and left the room. He sacrificed his camel and shaved his head. When the Muslims saw this, they got up and followed what he had done. The revelation left no doubt that their expedition had been a success for it opened with, *"Verily We have given you a clear victory."* (48:1) Umm Salamah had been a good wife and advisor to the Messenger of God.

IDENTIFICATIONS:
* **Banu Abd al-Asad**
* **Quba**
* **Ayyin al-Arab**
CONSIDER AND DISCUSS:
1. Discuss the help given Umm Salamah by the non-Muslim Quraysh.
2. Discuss Umm Salamah's advice to the Messenger which he accepted.

ABDULLAH IBN HUDHAYFAH:
The Courier

Abdullah ibn Hudhayfah had heard that one day, in preparing the trenches for the Battle of Khandaq, the Emigrants had needed help in splitting or dislodging a rock. Umar had gone to the Messenger for help and the Messenger had taken a pickax and struck the rock. As a result, a flare like lightning had flashed over the city towards the south. He struck again and again and it was as if lightning flashed but this time in the direction of Uhud towards the north and beyond. The Messenger struck a third time and a third time a light flashed and this time, eastwards. Salman saw the three flashes and realized they must have some special meaning. He asked the Messenger who said, "By the light of the first I saw the castles of the Yemen; by the light of the second I saw the castles of Syria; by the light of the third, I saw the white palace of Kisra at Mada'in. Through the first God opened up the Yemen to me; through the second, He has opened up Syria and the West; and through the third, the East." It was through these messages that Abdullah was destined to play an important role for Islam as a result of the Messenger of God wishing to spread the universal message he had been given. The time had come for the Messenger to spread the message of his mission beyond the borders of Arabia and to offer it to all of the people of the world.

The Messenger realized the great importance of this initiative. These envoys would be going to distant lands ruled by people who had no agreement with the Muslims. The envoys did not know the language of the rulers they would be inviting to Islam nor anything about their customs. They were to invite these rulers to give up their religion and their power to enter the faith of a people who not long before had been their subjects. The initiative was not without hazard.

The Messenger then sent letters to Khusrau, King of Persia which Abdullah carried; Heraclius, King of Rome; Hawzah, Ruler of Yamamah; to the Jews; and to the Bishop of Najran. The tone of these letters was serious and direct. There was the danger of a strong reaction to come from some of them. The Messenger was aware of this possibility. He prepared the letters while he continued to pursue his military and political options. To begin with, he removed all suspicious people from his ranks who could become a base in the event of a foreign attack. Also the minority religious community must be cleansed of anyone who could act as a fifth column internally and he sensed that this was the most immediate and sensitive act that a leader of a society was responsible for doing.

The letter to Heraclius, the King of Rome said: "In the Name of God, the Merciful, the Compassionate...I call upon you to submit to Islam. If you become a Muslim, you will share the Muslims' gains and their losses and if you do not want to become a Muslim yourself, then let your people freely convert to Islam or pay the poll tax, paid in lieu of conversion to Islam, and do not restrict them in choosing their faith."

The letter to the ruler of Yamamah said: "In the Name of God, the Merciful, the Compassionate. This is a letter from God's Messenger, Muhammad, to Hawzah. Greetings to the one who follows the path of salvation and the instructions of the divine guides. You, the ruler of Yamamah, note that my faith will advance to the farthest place where man can go, so submit to Islam to be immune."

A letter to the Jews said: "In the Name of God, the Merciful, the Compassionate. This is a letter from Muhammad, God's Messenger, Moses' brother and co-missionary. God has assigned to Muhammad the same mission He had assigned to Moses. I swear to you by God and by the sacred commands descended upon Moses on Mount Sinai that you have in your Holy Book, predictions of my prophetic mission to the Jewish community as well as to all other peoples. If you have found this, then fear God and convert to Islam, and if you have not found such a divine prediction, then you will be excused."

A letter to Bishop Najran said: "In the Name of God, the Merciful, the Compassionate. This is a letter from God's Prophet, Muhammad, to Bishop Najran. Truly I call on you to worship the real adored God instead of worshipping God's creatures."

Abdullah took the letter addressed to Khusrau Parviz in participating in this historic migration of the dissemination of thought and the extending of Islam among other lands and societies which the Messenger initiated by the sending of these letters. The Messenger was implementing his worldwide and universal mission which every Muslim believes in and also have a responsibility to carry out in order to bring awareness, consciousness, and freedom to all nations and races.

Preparing the things he would need for the long journey, Abdullah said good-by to his wife and son. He traveled long and far until he reached the capital of the Persian Empire. He asked for permission to enter the presence of the King as he had a message to deliver to him. He entered the royal audience hall and saw the King and his entourage dressed in the most expensive robes and wearing a great gem-studded turban. He himself was wearing the simple coarse clothes of the Muslims of Madinah, but he held his head high, honored by his faith.

As soon as the King saw him coming towards him, he summoned an aide to take the letter from Abdullah. Abdullah refused to give it to anyone but the King himself. Khusrau Parviz then gave him permission to step forward. Abdullah handed him the letter which said: "From Muhammad, God's Messenger, to Khusrau, the King of Persia. Peace be upon whoever follows the right guidance, to those obedient to God and His Prophet, to those who bear witness to God's Oneness, who worship the One God, and who bear witness to the prophecy of God's servant, Muhammad. Truly I call upon you to obey God's Command and convert to Islam. I am God's Messenger to all the people so that living hearts will be awakened and illuminated and so that infidels will have no excuses. Submit to Islam so you will be safe and immune and if you disobey me and turn down my invitation, you will be blamed for the sins of the magi."

The King summoned the Arab speaking clerk to come forward and translate. He began, "In the Name of God, the Merciful, the Compassionate. From Muhammad, Messenger of God, to Khusrau Parviz, the ruler of Persia. Peace be on whoever follows the right guidance..." The translator had only gotten this far when Khusrau Parviz's anger raged out of control. He seized the letter and tore it to sheds saying, "How dare he, my slave, address me so!" He was angry that the Prophet had not put his name first. He commanded Abdullah to be expelled from the audience hall.

Abdullah did not wait to see what would happen to him. He slipped away at the first opportunity and headed back for Madinah. When Khusrau Parviz had cooled down, he asked that the Messenger be brought before him. They searched everywhere and could not find Abdullah. They sent out a party to find him on his way back, but he was far ahead of them and they did not succeed.

Once he returned to Madinah, Abdullah told the Messenger about what had happened and how Khusrau Parviz tore up the letter before it was even read completely. The Messenger replied, "May God tear up his kingdom." Khusrau Parviz then sent orders to his ambassador in Yemen to send two men to Madinah and to escort the up-start who wrote the letter to Persia.

The two men set out to accomplish their task. At Taif they met some Quraysh traders and they asked them about Muhammad. They were told, "He is in Yathrib (Madinah)." They were pleased that they had so easily found his whereabouts. They first went to Makkah and told the Quraysh there that Khusrau Parviz was about to eliminate Muhammad and that then their worries would be over. The two men then left for Madinah. The two envoys, following the custom of the Persian court in those days, had shaved their heads and grown long mustaches. The Messenger was appalled when he saw them and asked, "Who told you to do this?"

"Our lord, Khusrau," they replied.

The Messenger said, "My Lord has told me to lengthen my beard and shorten my mustache." He then sent them away and told them to come back the next day. That night, Gabriel told him that Khusrau Parviz had been killed and his son was reigning in his place. When the envoys returned the next day, he told them to tell their governor, "My religion and empire will extend far beyond the Kingdom of Khusrau. Say to him from me: 'Accept Islam and I will confirm you in whatever you have. I will appoint you King over the Yemen.'"

They delivered the message. The governor said he would send a courier to find out if this news was true, but before he had a chance to do that, an envoy arrived with the news of the death of Khusrau Parviz and claiming his allegiance for the new King. Instead of accepting this, the governor and the two envoys accepted Islam and many other Persians did so as well. He sent word to the Messenger in Madinah and the Messenger confirmed his rule over the Yemen. This was the first of the three lights that were fulfilled.

Abdullah ibn Hudhayfah, the courier of this light, died during the caliphate of Umar ibn Khattab. May God rest his soul in peace.

IDENTIFICATIONS:
* Khusrau
* Heraclius
* Bishop Najran
CONSIDER AND DISCUSS:
1. Discuss the steps the Messenger of God took in case of a reaction from the world leaders when he invited them to Islam.
2. Discuss the contents of the letters sent by the Messenger of God to world leaders.

UMM HABIBAH:
A Woman Who Disobeys Her Apostate Husband

Umm Habibah or Ramlah was the daughter of Abu Sufyan and Hind, the leaders among the idol-worshipping multi-theists of Makkah and among those who continuously rebelled against God's Commands (*taghut*). Ramlah grew up in a home where the 'way of life' (*din*) was to worship multiple gods, deities who the carver-worshipper believed influenced their life and their fate, therefore they were considered to be sacred. The Quran, addressing them, said, *"Do you worship things which you (yourselves) carve?"* (37:95)

Her family believed itself to be a religious family because they were devoted to their idols. They invited others to rebel against the One God and because they followed a man-made system of surrender, they were enslaved by hundreds of other powers where each power or pole formed a class and each group had a deity.

Idolatry as a form of multitheism (*shirk*) means servitude to other than God and, at one and the same time, it means surrender and submission to one's enslavement to idols *"which they themselves carve."* This belief promotes oppression, ignorance, and deceit in order to justify the status quo —noble and ignoble, master and slave, abased and enslaving, ruler and ruled, captive and free.

Ramlah's parents believed that multiple gods must exist for the multiple levels of society so that there always be multiple classes and families. Then the strong, the ones with power, could abase and subjugate the weak, powerless, and deprived. And yet, Ramlah, growing up under this system, alone among her family, became, by the Grace of God, a monotheist (*muwwahid*). This is a person who believed in the Abrahamic Tradition confirmed by the Messenger of God (ص), that there is but One Power and one direction in creation, that all of the created world, whether animate or inanimate, is ruled by the One God and that other than He there is no cause. Hers is a faith which continuously appears against those who rebel against God's Commands (*taghut*) like her father, Abu Sufyan, before his conversion to Islam two years before the Messenger of God died. Monotheism stands behind the oppressed and the deprived as its goal is social justice. The religion of monotheism towards which Ramlah is guided is "submission to the Will of God,'" born of awareness, consciousness, and the need for love, worship, and praise of Allah.

Ramlah or Umm Habibah was one who struggled in God's Cause (*mujahid*), a pious, Muslim believing woman, a woman who did not let destructive courses, storms, and events or unexpected bitter moments shake her firm faith. She grew up inclined towards faith in the One God in spite of her circumstances. She became a model for people of faith, *"God is the protector of the believers. He brings them forth from the shadows into the light. And the unbelievers — their protectors are idols, that bring them forth from the light into the shadows..."* (2:2576) She was a woman who withstood the torture and persecution of the Quraysh in Makkah until the Messenger of God commanded those so punished to migrate. She went to Abyssinia with her husband.

Abyssinia was a Christian country and people there were able to practice their faith as they believed it should be practiced. The ceremonies of the Christian court of those days, on the one hand, and the attraction of the environment and Christian propaganda, on the other, could have been important factors in shaking the faith and beliefs of the Muslims causing them to become Christians.

But the Emigrants to Abyssinia, men and women alike, young and old, were strong in their faith. They were people who had been willing to give up everything they owned in order to practice their faith as they believed God had wanted. Yet, there is one among them one who lost his strength and his faith. He was Ubaydullah ibn Jahsh, the husband of Umm Habibah. He turned away from the Divine Law (*shariah*) and she found the strength to turn away from him, perhaps because she had seen in her own family where such a road leads.

Her life choice may have been inspired by the life of Asiyah, the wife of Pharaoh, one of the four perfect women mentioned by the Messenger of God. Asiyah was married to an arrogant, godless, and wicked man who refused to believe in Moses' mission. Asiyah achieved a great spiritual triumph when she preserved her faith, humility, and piety, having saved the life of the infant Moses. The Quran said, *"And God sets forth as an example for the believers — the wife of Pharaoh— when she said, 'My Lord! Build for me a house in Paradise in Your presence and save me from Pharaoh and his work and save me from those that do wrong"* (66:11). Asiyah's spiritual vision was directed towards God rather than to the worldly attachments and grandeur of Pharaoh's court. Her prayer implied that she sought martyrdom which she may have attained.

Umm Habibah contrasted with the examples in the Quran for the unbelievers when God said, *"God sets forth an example for the unbelievers — the wife of Noah and the wife of Lot for they were under two of Our righteous servants, but they betrayed them so they availed them nothing whatsoever against God; so it was said, 'Enter you two the Fire with those who enter.'"* (66:10). These two women betrayed their husbands who followed God's Commands and as each person has to account for themselves, they could not be saved simply because they were the wives of pious men. As there is a personal responsibility before God, no one can claim the merits of the other nor can one pure soul be injured by associating with a corrupt soul. The pure one should keep his/her purity intact as did Ramlah.

Or does her decision resemble the model for believers of Mary about which the Quran said, *"And Mary, the daughter of Imran, who guarded her chastity so We breathed into her of Our Spirit and she confirmed the Words of her Lord and of His Books and was one of the obedience"* (66:12) Mary had true faith to which she bore witness through her son, Jesus (﷿) and in his revelation as well as the revelations he came to confirm. She was among the believers, obedient, and devout, who have, throughout history, worshiped the One God. And God said, *"We appointed her and her son to be a Sign for all peoples. Surely, this community (ummah) of yours is a single community and I am your Lord so serve Me"* (21:91-92).

Umm Habibah's husband died as a result of his corrupt lifestyle and she was left alone in Abyssinia. She could not return to her parents, Abu Sufyan and Hind, as they were still among the leaders of all that she had struggled to attain. Yet, the pull towards them was naturally a strong one for her. Did not the Quran say, *"And those who strive in Our (cause) — We will certainly guide them to Our Paths for surely God is with those who do right"* (29:69). He had not forgotten her.

Sometime later she recorded that she had a dream in which someone calls her 'mother of the believers' (*umm muminun*). "I interpreted my dream," she said, "by realizing that I would marry the Messenger of God." A few days later the Negus sent an envoy to her who said, "The Messenger of Islam has asked that you marry him. Decide for yourself and if you agree, chose someone to act on your behalf and we will arrange the marriage ceremony."

She chose Khalid ibn Sa'id as her representative and, then, sensing how blessed she was, Umm Habibah gave all of her jewelry to the servant she had been given. The Negus invited Ja'far ibn Abi Talib, the leader of the Muslims in Abyssinia, and all the other Muslims, to a gathering and the marriage contract was signed.

With this marriage, the Messenger of God wanted to show woman like Umm Habibah who have sacrificed so much for her faith should not feel alone, but rather sense that there is some support like the Messenger of God who stood behind her. She wished to give all of her wedding presents to the female slave but the slave refused the gifts saying, "I receive gifts from the Negus. Know that I have become a Muslim. When you see the Messenger of God, give him my greetings." In CE 628/AH 7 Umm Habibah migrated to Madinah where she met the Messenger and told him about life in Abyssinia and the marriage ceremony. She also sent the greetings of the female salve to him and he blessed her.

Umm Habibah died in CE 644/AH 44, a pious, believing 'mother of the believers'. May God rest her soul in peace.

IDENTIFICATIONS:

* *shirk*

* *muwwahid*

* *mujahid*

CONSIDER AND DISCUSS:

1. Discuss the social system that develops from a belief in many gods or deities.

2. Discuss what a monotheistic society would be.

ZAYD IBN HARITHA:
The Standard Bearer of the Battle of Mut'ah

Sold into slavery at an early age, he was bought by a nephew of Khadijah, the wife of the Messenger of God. She gave him to her beloved Muhammad (ﷺ) before his mission. The Messenger then freed him and adopted him as his son so that he became known as Zayd ibn Muhammad until the verse "...*nor has He made your adopted sons your sons...Call them by (the names of) their fathers. That is more just in the sight of God...*" (33:4-5) was revealed. When Zayd's father learned that his son was alive, he went to Makkah to try to have his son return to his own people. Zayd was given the choice by Muhammad (ﷺ). He chose to stay with the Messenger but after the above verse was revealed, he used his father's family name, Haritha.

Zayd was one of the earliest converts to Islam. At the time of the migration to Madinah, he accompanied the Messenger's daughters, Fatimah and Umm Kulthum and the Messenger's wife after Khadijah's death, Sawda bint Zam'a. A brave warrior, he fought at Badr, Uhud, Khandaq, and was at Hudaybiah. He was made the commander of the forces for the Battle of Mu'tah in September CE 629/AH 8 where he was martyred. The memories of the *mujahid* in this battle have been preserved in poetry from that time.

The Messenger sent Zayd as the commander to Mu'tah. He said that if Zayd was slain, Ja'far ibn Abi Talib was to be in command, and if he was killed, Abdullah ibn Rawahah should lead the forces. The expedition prepared 3,000 men for the confrontation with the forces of Heraclius, the Byzantine emperor. When the army was about to set of, they said farewell to the Messenger's chiefs and saluted them. When Abdullah ibn Rawahah took his leave of the chiefs, he wept and when they asked him the reason, he said, "By God, it is not that I love the world and am inordinately attached to you, but I heard the Messenger read a verse from the Quran in which he mentions hell: *'There is not one of you but shall come to it; that is a determined decree of your Lord,'* (19:72) and I do not know how I can return after I have been to it.' The Muslims said, "God be with you and protect you and bring you back to us safe and sound."

Abdullah said:

> But I ask the Merciful's pardon
> And a wide open wound discharging blood,
> Or a deadly lance-thrust from a zealous warrior
> That will piece the bowels and liver;
> So that men will say when they pass my grave,
> 'God guide him, fine raider that he was, he died well.'

Then the people marched with the army to the edge of the city, the Messenger with them, said their farewells and returned.

Abdullah said:

> May peace remain on the best companion and friend,
> The man I said good-bye to amid the palms.

The army went as far as Ma'an in Syria when they heard that

Heraclius had come to a nearby city with 100,000 Byzantines who had been joined by 100,000 men from Lakhm and Judham. When the Muslims heard this, they spent two nights in Ma'an discussing what they should do. They discussed writing the Messenger and telling him of the enemy's numbers. If he sent reinforcements, well and good, and if not, they would await his orders. Abdullah ibn Rawahah encouraged the men saying, "Men, what you dislike is that which you have come out in search of (martyrdom). We are not fighting the enemy with numbers or strength or multitude, but we are confronting them with this religion with which God has honored us. So come on! Both prospects are fine: victory or martyrdom." The men responded, "By God, Ibn Rawahah is right."

The Muslims went forward until when they were on the borders of the Balqa where the forces of Heraclius met them in a village called Masharif. When the enemy approached, the Muslims withdraw to a village called Mu'tah. When the fighting began, Zayd ibn Haritha fought holding the Messenger's standard until he died from loss of blood among the spears of the enemy. Then Ja'far ibn Abu Talib took over and fought until he was martyred. When Ja'far was martyred, Abdullah ibn Rawahah, who was from the Helpers, took the standard and advanced. He had to put pressure on himself as he felt reluctant to go forward. Then he said:

> I swear, my soul, you shall come to the battle;
> You shall fight or be made to fight.
> Though men shout and scream aloud,
> Why should you spurn Paradise:
> Long have you been at ease.
> You are nothing but a drop in a worn-out skin.

According to the Traditions, when the army was attacked like this, the Messenger said to his companions, "Zayd took the standard and fought with it until he was killed as a martyred; then Ja'far took it and fought until he was killed as a martyr." Then he was silent until the faces of the helpers fell. They think that something disastrous had happened to Abdullah ibn Rawahah. Then the Messenger continued, "Abdullah took it and fought by it until he was killed as a martyr. I saw in a vision that they were carried up to me in Paradise upon beds of gold."

Among the lamentations over the martyrdom of the Messenger's companions at Mu'tah, Hasan ibn Thabit wrote:

A miserable night I had in Yathrib,
Anxiety then robbed me of sleep when others slept soundly.
At the thought of a friend my tears ran fast.
(Memory is oft the cause of weeping.
Nay, the loss of a friend is a calamity.
And how many a noble soul is afflicted and endures patiently.)
I saw the best of the believers follow one another to death,
Though some held back behind them.
May God receive the slain at Mu'tah who
    went one after another.
Among them Ja'far now borne on wings,
And Zayd and Abdullah when they too followed
When the cords of death were active
On the day they went on with the believers,
The fortunate radiant one leading them to death.
Bright as the full moon—Hashim's sons,
Haughty against wrong, daringly bold,
He fought until he fell unpillowed
On the battlefield, a broken shaft in his body.
He has his reward with the martyrs,
Gardens and green spreading trees.
We saw in Ja'far a man loyal to Muhammad
One who gave decisive orders.
May there ever be in Islam of Hashim's line
Pillars of strength and an endless source of pride...

Mourning Zayd ibn Haritha and Abdullah ibn Rawahah, he said:

O eye, be generous with the last drop of thy tears

And remember as they ease those in their graves.
Remember Mu'tah and what happened there
When they went to their defeat,
When they returned leaving Zayd there.
Happy be the abode of the poor one, imprisoned (in the grave)
The friend of the best of all creatures,
The lord of men whose love fills their breasts.
Ahmad who has no equal,
My sorrow and my joy are for him.
Zayd's position with us
Was not that of a man deceived.
Be generous with thy tears for the Khazrajite,
He was a chief who gave freely there.
We have suffered enough by their death
And pass the night in joyless grief.

IDENTIFICATIONS:
* **Battle of Mut'ah**
* **Sawda bint Zam'a**
CONSIDER AND DISCUSS:
1. Discuss what the Muslims should have done when faced with an overwhelming enemy.
2. Why did the Quran not allow an adopted son to take the name of his adopted father?

A'ISHAH BINT ABU BAKR:
A Transmitter of Traditions

The beloved wife of the Messenger of God who he referred to lovingly as Humayra, A'ishah was a young woman when her husband died and the Quran had forbidden the wives of the Messenger ever marrying again. Known for her beauty and intelligence, she transmitted thousands of Traditions of the Messenger to history. Many of the learned companions and their followers benefited from her vast knowledge.

Her wedding to the Messenger of God was the simplest kind. She wore a dress made of red-striped cloth from Bahrain. Her mother took her to her new home. They brought a bowl of milk. The Messenger drank from it and offered it to her to drink. She declined but he persisted. Finally she offered the bowl to her half-sister, Asma, who was sitting beside her. Others also drank of it and that was the simple and solemn occasion of her wedding. There was no feast.

Later she said to the Messenger, "Compare your love for me with something."

He replied, "Like the rope's knot," meaning it is strong and secure. Time and time again after that she would ask him, "How is the knot?" And he would reply, "In the same condition."

She loved the Messenger so much that she would often became unhappy when his attention was given to others. She herself commented on this in later years, saying, "I was not as jealous of any other wife of the Messenger's as I was of Khadijah because of his constantly mentioning her and because God had commanded him to give her good tidings of a mansion in Paradise made of precious stones. And whenever he sacrificed a sheep, he would send a fair portion of it to those who had been her intimate friends. Many a time I said to him, 'It is as if there had never been any other woman in the world except Khadijah.'

"Once when I complained and asked why he spoke so highly of 'an old Quraysh woman,' the Messenger became very hurt and said, 'She was the wife who believed in me while others rejected me. When people called me a liar, she affirmed my truthfulness. When I stood forsaken, she spent her wealth to lighten the burden of my sorrow.'"

A'ishah was to bear all the hardships of poverty and hunger which often enveloped the Messenger's home. For days on end no fire would be lit in the simply furnished home of the Messenger to cook or bake bread. They lived on dates and water. Poverty did not distress A'ishah or humiliate her.

Once after the Battle of Khaybar, the Messenger absented himself from his wives for one month because they had distressed him by asking for things he did not have. Returning from this self-imposed retreat, he first went to A'ishah's house. She was delighted to see him but he said he has received two revelations which required him to place two options before her and his other wives. He then recited the verses, "*Oh Prophet of God! Say to your wives: If you desire the life of this world and its adornments, then come and I will bestow its goods upon you and I will release you with a fair re-lease. But if you desire God and His Messenger and the abode of the Hereafter, then verily God has laid in store for you an immense reward for such as you who do good"* (33:28).

A'ishah replied, "Indeed, I desire God and His Messenger and the abode of the Hereafter."

Among the Traditions she transmitted are those related to the Farewell Pilgrimage (*hajjat al-wida*) of the Messenger of God. The great mission of the Messenger of God was coming to a close. It was the tenth year since the migration began. The first thing was to say good-by to the people: in Makkah, beside the House of God and the people, the Kabah. Two months before it was announced to all Muslims that whoever wanted to perform the pilgrimage with the Messenger should go to Madinah and from there, they would all move together to the Kabah.

This was the first pilgrimage of the Messenger. It was the first time that more than 100,000 had set up tents outside Madinah in order to move with the Messenger of God towards Makkah. And, it was the Messenger's Farewell or last pilgrimage, as well.

On the 25th of Dhiqadeh, they left Madinah. The Messenger took all of his wives with him. They stayed the night in Dhu 'l-Halifah and early in the morning, put on the pilgrim's garb and began to move, praying throughout the way, *"Yea, oh Lord. Yea. Praise and blessings belong to Thee and dominion! There is no partner for Thee. Yea."* The words echoed through the desert.

Under the scorching sun of the peninsula, over the scorched earth, for the first time in history, Muslims moved toward one *qiblah*. There was no sign of color, rank, decoration, or formalities. All was one color: white. Clothes were all two things: one cloth worn over the shoulders and one cloth wrapped around the waist. Here the show of beauty was the colorless life of the human being. The drama was before society. No one should recognize the other person. It was forbidden for men to sew the cloth so that there be no way of distinguishing one from the other. Here all

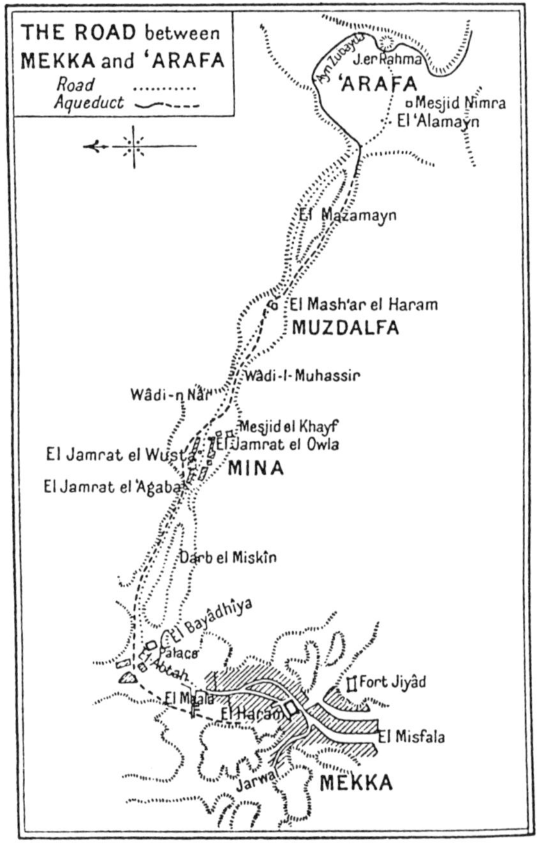

were human beings and nothing else. Colors and signs were all thrown away in Dhu 'l-Halifah.

The Messenger moved the Muslims—one color, one dress—along with him. History which is used to recording the activities of the royal court, palaces of Kings, Sultans, and Pharaohs is obliged, here, to fix itself on these sacrifices of poverty, anguish, and oppression.

The 4th of Dhihijjah they entered Makkah. Here all were gathered: God, Abraham, the Kabah, Muhammad (ص) and the people. The Messenger had come to the Station of Abraham, the great idol-destroyer in humanity and history, to offer to God the fruits of his amazing work the last few days of his life. At His threshold he wanted the people to bear witness to the fact that he undertook every effort possible to fulfill his mission. He wanted to teach tomorrow's history that this was what an *'ummah'* is; that future human life on the earth be as this; and finally, to speak to the people as a whole for the last time—to see them and to bid them farewell and end the wondrous story of these beloved shepherds who continuously appeared out of the desert and arose against the gods of gold and the gods of power.

After the circumambulation, in the Station of Abraham, they recited two cycles of the ritual prayer, kissed the Black Stone twice, and then immediately moved towards Safa and walked between Safa and Marwah. At this point it was announced, whoever does not have an animal to sacrifice, should perform the shorter hajj and remove the pilgrim's clothes. This was an extremely difficult thing for many of the Muslims to do and they had doubts about it. The Messenger became angry and it showed on his face. In words which shook from his anger, he said, "Do whatever I command you to do."

A'ishah fearfully asked, "Who has made you so angry?" He answered, "Why should I not get upset. I tell them to do something and they don't listen." A companion entered and the Messenger could see he was very sad. With great sorrow, he said, "Oh Messenger of God, whoever has angered you will be punished by God in the fire." The Messenger said, "Did you not see how I gave an order and the people doubted it. If I had known, I also would not have brought an animal to sacrifice so that, like them, I would have removed my pilgrim's clothes."

The people realized the Messenger was unhappy. They were ashamed of what they had done. They quickly took off their pilgrim's clothes. Fatimah, the Messenger's daughter did so and all the women with her who did not bring a sacrifice with them, did the same. That night when the Messenger visited A'ishah in her tent, he found her weeping. She was in a state of ritual impurity and could not perform the rites. She said, "I told him what my problem was and said I wished to God that I had not come out with him on the journey this year. He said, 'Do not say that for you can do all that the pilgrims do except circumambulate the Kabah,'" which she did and later did the circumambulation.

On the 8th of Dhihijjah they went to Mina. The morning of the next day the Messenger of God went to Arafah. The sun reached its noon peak and rained down on people's heads. The Messenger sat upon litters piled one upon another amidst the people—men and women—who gathered around him from everywhere. Rabi'ah, the brother of Safwan, was made responsible to repeat whatever it was that the Messenger said because of his powerful voice. Everyone must hear what he had to say. All the words should reach as many as possible.

Everything seemed out of the ordinary; the moment chosen for these words, the place, the situation and condition of the Messenger and, in particular, the special style of his words.

The Messenger began, "The Messenger of God says: Say what month this is?" They were silent and he answered, "The sacred month." Then he asked, "Say what land this is?" Again they were silent and he answered, "The sacred land." Then he asked, "What day is this?" And again he answered, "The day of the Longer Pilgrimage." Then he said and Rabi'ah repeated, "Verily God has made inviolable for you each other's blood and each other's property until you meet your Lord, even as He has made inviolable this your day, in this your land, in this your month."

Then he began his sermon, "Oh people, listen to my words. I do not know whether I shall ever meet you again in this place after this year. Your blood and your property are sacred until you meet your Lord. As this day and this month are sacred, you will surely meet your Lord and He will ask you of the words I have told you. He who has a pledge, let him return it to him who entrusted him with it. All usury is abolished, but you have your capital. Do not oppress others nor be oppressed. God has decreed that there is to be no usury and the usury of Abbas ibn Abd al-Muttalib is abolished, all of it. All bloodshed in the pagan period is to be left unavenged. The first claim on blood I abolish is that of ibn Rabi'ah ibn al-Harith ibn Abd al-Muttalib. It is the first bloodshed in the pagan period that I overlook.

"Oh people! Satan despairs of ever being worshiped in your land, but if he can be obeyed in anything short of worship, he will be pleased in matters you may be disposed to think of little account, so beware of his presence in your way of life.

"Oh people! Postponement of a sacred month is only an excess of disbelief whereby those who disbelieve are misled; they allow it one year and forbid it another year that they may make up the number of months which God has made sacred, so that they permit what God has forbidden, and forbid what God has allowed. Time has completed its cycle and it is as if it was on the days that God created the heavens and the earth. The number of months with God are twelve; four of them are sacred, three consecutive and Rajab of Mundar which is between Jumada and Sha'ban.

"Oh people! you have rights over your wives and they have rights over you. You have the right that they shall not commit adultery and that they should not behave with open unseemliness. If they do, God allows you to put them in separate rooms and discipline them. If they refrain from these things, give them food and clothing with kindness. You have taken them as a trust from God and made them permissible through the Words of God. Understand, then, oh people, what I am saying.

"Oh people! As I have told you, I have left something to which if you will hold fast, you will never fall into error—a clear Sign—the Book of God and the practice of His Prophet, so heed well what I say.

"Oh people, know that every Muslim is another Muslim's brother and all Muslims are brothers. It is only lawful to take from a brother what he gives you willingly so do not oppress yourselves."

At this moment under the burning sun, while it seemed as if he had just completed his mission, he raised his eyes to the heavens and asked, "Oh God, have I conveyed it?"

The people said, "Oh God, yes," and the Messenger said, "Oh God, bear witness."

"I have left amongst you that which, if you hold fast to it, shall preserve you from all error, a clear indication, the Book of God and the word of His Prophet. Oh people, hear my words and understand. *'This day the unbelievers despair of prevailing against your religion, so fear them not, but fear Me!! This day have I perfected for you your religion and fulfilled My favor not you, and it has been My good pleasure to choose Islam for you as your religion'* (5:3)."

It was not long after the return of the Messenger from the pilgrimage when he sensed death approaching. His wives suggested that he go to A'ishah's house. For most of the time he lay there on the couch with his head resting on her lap and that was where he died, peace and the blessings of God be upon him. A'ishah lived a long life after the death of her beloved husband, dying in CE 678/AH 58. May Allah rest her soul in peace.

IDENTIFICATIONS:
* *hajjat al-wida*
* *qiblah*
CONSIDER AND DISCUSS:
1. Discuss why the Messenger was angered by the people's lack of response to his command.
2. How did the Messenger show his love for A'ishah?

Bibliography

Abu al-Faraj al-Isfahani. *Kitab al-aghani*. Cairo: al-Hay'ah al-mis-
riyyah al-'ammah li-al-ta'lif wa-al-nashr, 1963.
al-Khatib al-Tibrizi. *Mishkat al-Masabih*. Translated by James
Robson. 4 vols. Lahore, 1963-65.
al-Tabari, Abu Ja'far Muhammad b. Jarir. *Ta'rikh al-rusul wa-al-
muluk*, 43 vols. New York: SUNY Press, 1987-.
al-Tabari. *Annales*. Edited by M. de Goeje and J. Barth. 8 vols.
Leiden: Brill, 1879-1901. 2nd ed. Cairo, 1939.
An-Nawawi, Yahya bin Sharaf ud-Din. *Riyad as-Salihin*, 2 vols.
Chicago: Library of Islam, 1988.
Athar, Alia. *Prophets: Models for Humanity*. Chicago: Library
of Islam, 1993.
Bakhtiar, Laleh. *History of Islam*. Chicago: Library of Islam,
1993
Bemat, M. A. E. *Shamail-i-Tirmizi*. Chicago: Library of Islam,
Inc., 1985.
Bukhari, Muhammad ibn Ismail al-. *Sahih al-Bukhari*, 9 vols.
Chicago: Library of Islam, 1979.
Dodge, B., ed. and trans. *The Fihrist of al-Nadim: A Tenth-Century
Survey of Muslim Culture*. 2 vols. New York: Columbia
University Press, 1970.
Encyclopedia of Islam. 1st ed. Leiden: E. J. Brill, 1913-36
Encyclopedia of Islam. 2nd ed. Leiden: E. J. Brill, 1960-.
Hasan, Ahmad. *Sunan Abu Dawud*. 3 vols. Chicago: Library
of Islam, 1988.
Haykal, Muhammad. *Life of Muhammad*. Indiana: NAIT, 1976.
Ibn al-Athir, 'Izz al-Din. *al-Kamil fi al-ta'rikh*, ed. C. Tornberg. 13
vols. Leiden: E. J. Brill, 1867. Repr. Beirut: Dar Sadir, 1965.
Ibn Hajar al-'Asqalani. *Tahdhib al-tahdhib*. Hyderabad: n.p., 1325-
27/1907-8.
Ibn Ishaq. *Sirat Rasul Allah*, trans. A. Guillaume. Oxford
University Press, 1987.
Ibn Khaldun, 'Abd al-Rahman b. Muhammad. *al-Muqaddimah*,
trans. F. Rosenthal as *The Muqaddimah: An Introduction to
History*. 3 vols. Bollingen Series XLVIII. New York: Pantheon
Press, 1958.
Ibn Sa'd, Abu Abdullah Muhammad. *Kitab al-tabaqat al-kabir*, ed.
E. Sachau as *Biographien Muhammeds*. 9 vols. Leiden: E. J. Brill,

1904-21.

Kandhlawi, M. M. Y. *Hayatus Sahabah: The Lives of the Sahabah*, 2 vols. Chicago: Library of Islam, 1991.

Khatib al-Tibrizi, Muhammad b. 'Abdallah. *Mishkat al-masabih*, trans. J. Robson. 2 vols. Lahore: Sh. Muhammad Ashraf, 1981.

Lane, E. W. *Arabic-English Lexicon*. 8 vols. London, 1863. Reprint. London, 1983.

Lings, M. *Muhammad his life based on the earliest sources*. Vermont: Inner Traditions, 1983.

Muslim, Imam. *Sahih Muslim*. 4 vols. Chicago: Library of Islam, Inc., 1990.

Numani, A. S. *Sirat un-Nabi*. 2 vols. Chicago: Library of Islam, Inc. 1979.

Rahman, Afzalur. *Encyclopedia of Seerah*. London, Seerah Foundation, 1982

Shorter Encyclopedia of Islam. Edited by H. A. R. Gibb and J. H. Kramers. Leiden: E. J. Brill, 1961.

Siddiqui, Abdul Hameed. *Life of Muhammad*. Chicago: Library of Islam, 1991.

Waheed ud-Din, F. S. *The Benefactor and the Rightly-guided*. Chicago: Library of Islam, 1992.

Watt, W. M. *Muhammad in Mecca*. Oxford: Oxford University Press, 1953.

Watt, W. M. *Muhammad in Medina*. Oxford: Oxford University Press, 1962.

Books on this Subject Recommended for Children

Ahmad, Fazl. *Some Stories of the Companions*. 3 vols. Lahore: Sh. Ashraf, 1985.

Athar, Alia N. *Muhammad, the Last Messenger*. 2 vols. Chicago: Library of Islam, 1992.

Athar, Alia N. *Muhammad, the Last Prophet*. 2 vols. Chicago: Library of Islam, 1992.

Murad, Khurram. *Stories of the Broken Idol and the Jewish Rabbi*. London: Islamic Foundation, 1985.

Murad, Khurram. *Stories of the Caliphs*. London: Islamic Foundation, 1983.

Murad, Khurram. *The Wise Poet*. London: Islamic Foundation, 1985.

General Index

A

B